In a day when absolutes are few and the overall religious trend is moving toward a God who is self-defined and self-serving, it is refreshing to read a book so solidly founded on the absolute truth of God's Word. The reader will more fully understand that God didn't give suggestions, and He didn't give a list of do's and don'ts, but as a loving Father God, He gave direction for living life to the fullest . . . His way of life.

Rick Kingham
Vice-President of Worship, Promise Keepers

Glen Martin illustrates and applies the timeless truths of the Ten Commandments in a timely manner to a new generation. In our mixed-up world of beliefs, ethics, and morals, God's Top Ten List *is TOP-NOTCH! It is a fresh review of age-old truth.*

Dr. Gary L. McIntosh, Professor
Talbot School of Theology, Biola University

I speak to groups of men every month and challenge them to raise the standard of moral and spiritual virtue and set an example in the very matters Glen highlights in this book. It is a book I'll consistently recommend to those who attend the conferences I lead. Both men and women will appreciate Glen's writing style. This book makes my "top ten list."

Jim Neal
President/CEO
Dad the Family Shepherd

Dr. Glen Martin demonstrates again why he is one of America's leading pastors and speakers. God's Top Ten List *takes the ancient truths of the Ten Commandments and shows their relevance and power for the church of the twenty-first century. In an exciting and highly readable presentation, Dr. Martin lets us know that the Word of God of yesterday is still the Word of God today.*

Thom S. Rainer, Dean
Billy Graham School of Missions
Evangelism and Church Growth

For the biblically literate, the challenge is presenting the old in a new and relevant light. Little is older than the Ten Commandments, yet Glen Martin accomplishes this challenge. It is must reading for those whose familiarity breeds contempt.

Charles Cooper
National Director, Sign Ministries

In his unique and powerful way, Dr. Martin calls his readers to examine their relationship to the God of the List. Perhaps the best test of a book and its author is whether or not the reader is called to a life changed by what he or she reads. You cannot read this book and remain unchanged. Now please excuse me while I make a long overdue call to correct some words spoken in . . . well, anger. Thanks, Glen.

Bert Downs, President
Western Seminary

Glen Martin steps out of a world of moral relevancy and individual definitions of "right" and "wrong" and describes for the modern mind the will of God. The truth of this book gives the reader the deepest of spiritual experiences . . . what God looks like when He lives in His creation . . . you and me.

Dr. Conrad Lowe
Executive Minister
American Baptist Churches of the West

I once read that if you are a person of principle, then 99 percent of your decisions are already made before entering any situation. I have found that perspective leads to priorities and priorities lead to practice. Yet, what determines your perspective? If you are a Christian, then it is very simple—it's the Ten Commandments. Glen Martin has written a fresh, creative, and practical approach to living out these commandments—God's Top Ten List. These timeless principles are couched in everyday practical settings and terminology that allow the reader to embrace life by the throat and live it fully as God has intended.

Dr. Rodney L. Cooper,
Denver Seminary

God's Top Ten List

the ten commandments

Glen S. Martin

MOODY PRESS
CHICAGO

To Mary Cohick,
the mother of my wife,
grandmother to my children,
and loving example to me.

You always have and always will be
a tremendous influence in our lives.
Thank you for modeling
Jesus' love, mercy, and
servant's heart.
You have been the wind beneath our wings!
WE LOVE YOU!

Contents

Foreword

There is a frightening loss of our historical biblical heritage in today's culture. Many now believe there is no such thing as absolute truth, and that everything is relative. People have become a law unto themselves, rejecting the ancient principles upon which our nation and, indeed, civilization in general, was founded. Moral anarchy reigns in much of the nation and the world. Because of that, we have seen a shocking breakdown in the family and in society, and meteoric increases in crime and other measures of social disintegration.

So how refreshing it is to see a reemphasis on God's commandments, such as so beautifully provided by Dr. Martin! Because God is full of mercy and loving-kindness, we learn that His commandments are not burdensome nor arbitrary, but are given totally for our benefit. They are given as acts of kindness by our great and loving God to help us and to keep us from destroying ourselves and our societies.

We ignore God's commandments at our peril, often

death. But we find blessings when we obey them. It is as simple as that.

The Bible says that when sin abounds, grace does much more abound. In spite of the great evil around us, I believe a fresh wind of the Spirit is blowing. Revival is in the air. People are being supernaturally touched and are being drawn by the Holy Spirit to an awareness of who Jesus is, their sin, and their emptiness without Him.

I pray that this book will touch many, presently in darkness, but who are being drawn by the Spirit of God to salvation and a close walk in the Spirit. I also pray it will touch many present believers with a fresh awareness of the total relevance of God's commandments—not from a legalistic standpoint, but as God's vehicle for setting us free and blessing us with His wisdom for living.

People have a choice of death (ignoring God's commandments) or life (obeying them). There really is no choice. We must choose life.

DR. BILL BRIGHT, FOUNDER AND PRESIDENT
CAMPUS CRUSADE FOR CHRIST INTERNATIONAL

Acknowledgments

In writing a book there are many people who influence the author and make the book a reality. First of all, I would like to thank my wife, Nancy, for the number of hours she has spent typing and correcting and sharing her personal touch. A special thanks to Kerry, Scott, and David, our three children, who have put up with long hours with dad at the computer.

Thank you, Community Baptist Church staff, for not only living *God's Top Ten List,* but also being willing to give me input, encouragement, and continued motivation.

Thank you, Gary McIntosh, for always motivating me to put my thoughts onto paper. Your example as a change agent and champion of the church has been inspirational to me throughout my ministry.

Last, but certainly not least, I must thank Jim Bell for believing in me and Anne Scherich, whose creative flair has brough life and vitality to this manuscript. Thank you for being so patient with me. You have been a joy to work with.

loving **GOD** and worshiping Him

Hearing that Jesus had silenced the Sadducees, the Pharisees got together. One of them, an expert in the law, tested him with this question: "Teacher, which is the greatest commandment in the law?"

Jesus replied: "'Love the Lord your God with all your heart and with all your soul and with all your mind.' This is the first and greatest commandment. And the second is like it: 'Love your neighbor as yourself.' All the Law and the Prophets hang on these two commandments."

—Matthew 22:34–40

chapter one

God's
Top Ten
List

*And God spoke all these words: "I am the Lord your God,
who brought you out of Egypt, out of the land of slavery."*
—Exodus 20:1–2

David Letterman has popularized the use of top ten
lists. He is ruthless in his endeavor to poke fun and ex-
pose weaknesses. But the original expression of this
phenomenon began a long time ago—when God Himself offered a very different Top Ten List, which we call
the Ten Commandments.

GOD'S TOP TEN LIST (EXODUS 20:2–17 NIV)

1. *I am the Lord your God, who brought you out of
   Egypt, out of the land of slavery. You shall have no
   other gods before me* (vv. 2–3).

2. *You shall not make for yourself an idol in the form of
   anything in heaven above or on the earth beneath or
   in the waters below. You shall not bow down to them
   or worship them; for I, the Lord your God, am a jealous God, punishing the children for the sin of the fathers to the third and fourth generation of those who*

hate me, but showing love to a thousand generations of those who love me and keep my commandments (vv. 4–6).

3. *You shall not misuse the name of the Lord your God, for the Lord will not hold anyone guiltless who misuses his name (v. 7).*

4. *Remember the Sabbath day by keeping it holy. Six days you shall labor and do all your work, but the seventh day is a Sabbath to the Lord your God. On it you shall not do any work, neither you, nor your son or daughter, nor your manservant or maidservant, nor your animals, nor the alien within your gates. For in six days the Lord made the heavens and the earth, the sea, and all that is in them, but he rested on the seventh day. Therefore the Lord blessed the Sabbath day and made it holy (vv. 8–11).*

5. *Honor your father and your mother, so that you may live long in the land the Lord your God is giving you (v. 12).*

6. *You shall not murder (v. 13).*

7. *You shall not commit adultery (v. 14).*

8. *You shall not steal (v. 15).*

9. *You shall not give false testimony against your neighbor (v. 16).*

10. *You shall not covet your neighbor's house. You shall not covet your neighbor's wife, or his manservant or maidservant, his ox or donkey, or anything that belongs to your neighbor (v. 17).*

But why another book on the Ten Commandments? I'll tell you why. We are living in an age of moral crisis, and our culture is being reshaped by degenerating mind-sets.

THREE PHILOSOPHIES
MOLDING OUR CULTURE

Many people are looking today for morality lite, everything you've ever wanted in a culture and less. No absolutes, no guidelines, and certainly no command- ments: "At least let me choose which commandments I like and agree with." How did we get here? Let me sug- gest three distinct philosophies reshaping our culture.

Secularism

To mention the idea of secularism in a book like this causes the hair on the back of some necks to stand on end. But secularism simply represents a philosophy of life in which the ultimate determiner of truth is rational thought. *Webster's* defines secularism as "indifference to or rejection or exclusion of religion and religious con- siderations."[1] A secular culture is one that has pushed religion to the side. There is no religious basis for laws or moral standards. Laws are "right" because they seem rational and fulfill an immediate need, not because they follow God's commandments for right living. So, if I tell a person what the Bible says about some important is- sue, that person might respond by saying something like, "That's good for you, but what does the Bible have to do with me? I go with what I think is logical and based on serious thinking."

It is thus a secular worldview that establishes secu- lar values. "Values govern our underlying thoughts, atti- tudes and decisions which result in behavior."[2] The Bible confirms the connection between our thoughts and our actions when it says, "As he thinketh in his heart, so is he" (Proverbs 23:7 KJV).

Pluralism

Christian apologist Ravi Zacharias defines *pluraliza-tion,* or *pluralism,* as "the existence and availability of a number of world-views, each vying for the allegiance of individuals, with no single world-view dominant."[3] In other words, everyone's convictions, views, and truth are equal. You have your view and I have my view. Both are equal in pluralism. Pluralism has affected religion too. That is why many religious accept many paths to God. No one way is seen as being the only truth. All philoso-phies and religions "contain" truth in the pluralistic mind-set.

This kind of pluralism is everywhere today. George Hunter writes: "Western Culture, as Ken Chafin observes, is much like ancient Athens where, in Acts 17, Paul rea-soned with people influenced by a range of religions and philosophies—from Epicureanism and Stoicism, to var-ious Gnostic and Mystery religions, to the cult of the Emperor . . . [T]he late 1980's saw the 'New Age' move-ment on the crest of a wave."[4]

We as a society have strayed from absolutes. Moral relativism is the rule of the day. We have all heard one or more of the following statements:

- What's true for you may not be true for me.
- One person's art is another person's pornography.
- There are no objective morals, just differing opinions.
- If it feels good, do it.
- Anything goes as long as you don't hurt anyone.
- No culture is better or worse than any other.

That's the problem. The foundations of truth have been washed away by the currents of pluralism. The waves are so strong we can't tell right from wrong any longer.

When you have no absolute standard against which to judge the accuracy of something, you end up with chaos. Consider what would happen to our space program if its leaders changed from an exact science of absolute truths to one of relativism. If they had several choices for how many miles it is to the moon, if they could not accurately calculate the consumption of fuel, or if they did not know the speed needed to land safely on the moon, Neil Armstrong would not have been able to take his "one small step for [a] man, one giant leap for mankind."

What if, during their return, one astronaut had talked the crew members into using different statistics for their calculations? They would be space dust by now! It is interesting how in science we demand exact, provable facts, but in interhuman relationships we set aside such requirements, sometimes even going in the opposite direction. Too often in society we are told there can be absolutely no absolutes.

Privatization

By *privatization* I simply mean that you keep your truth to yourself and I will do the same. In this mind-set, differences are private things, so I should never invade your right to hold your own opinion by trying to persuade you to my point of view. Norman Geisler, one of the nation's leading writers in the field of ethics, addresses the issue of abortion. "The pro-abortionist's self-designation as 'pro-choice' places emphasis on the right of the mother to decide whether she wants to have a baby or not. It reveals the belief that the right to privacy is dominant in the decision."[5]

A student who tells a friend, "Cheating is not right," may be confronted with, "Mind your own business." A fellow worker who takes home office supplies, and is caught, rationalizes, "You worry about your job; I'll take care of mine." Even family reunions are preprogrammed never to talk about politics and religion. Why? Religion is seen as a private issue. "You have your beliefs; I have mine. You believe what you want, and I'll believe what I want." Because we have become a secular society committed to keeping the peace at all costs by maintaining an egalitarian approach to truth and keeping it private, we have drifted into an age of "truth decay," and choices have become even more difficult.

THREE OPTIONS FOR LIVING

Life is a series of decisions. Everywhere you turn, you are immediately confronted with choices. How you make your decisions and the foundation for every one of your choices affects all areas of life. F. LaGard Smith, in his book *When Choice Becomes God,* talks about a "new revolution" now under way. He points out that this new revolution is based upon "the right for us to decide for ourselves, and the right of others to decide for themselves."[6]

If making decisions is so important, then each person must decide from the following three options how to live.

- Will I buy into my own game plan and do the best I can to struggle through life, recognizing that failures are simply a part of the process? This option gives me the right to fail without guilt, because it says failure is inevitable. This option also mini-mizes the downside of failure, since failure be-comes unavoidable. Many baby boomers buy into this option because they want to be without re-straint, free to determine their own fate.

- Will I play "follow-the-leader," choosing to walk in someone else's footsteps, acknowledging I may end up living in the other person's shadow throughout my life? I see this happen a lot in the ministry. In a media-dominated culture, where people in church constantly expect the best preaching, the best music, and the best dramas, church leaders begin to mimic the programming or style of the "successful" churches in our coun-try. When I get to heaven, God is not going to ask me, "Why weren't you more like Chuck Swindoll or Charles Stanley?" He's going to ask me, "Why weren't you more like Jesus?" With the option of following another, I may reduce the risk of failure, but I also produce more frustration as I stifle or weaken any natural abilities I have.

- Will I follow God's program, His guidelines for life? In this option, failure is not fatal if I follow God's guidelines and submit to and follow His will in all things.

What's your perspective on God's Top Ten List right now? Are you indifferent? Maybe you see this list as "guilt producers." You view them as merely a list of "Thou shalt nots!" Or maybe you are like many who see them as God's way of keeping us under His thumb and spoiling our fun. My guess is that the vast majority of our culture sees this Top Ten List as irrelevant. "What did God know about my life, my situation, my trials

3,500 years ago?" You'd be surprised. The next eleven chapters of this book will demonstrate not only their relevance to your life but will show that the Ten Commandments are timeless, wise principles from the very mouth of God. These principles can still show us how to live better as we catapult into the twenty-first century.

A LITTLE HISTORY

It was the third day of the third month some 3,500 years ago. God had delivered a ragtag bunch of slaves from the oppression of one of the greatest political and military powers of the day. And not without a fight. Upon their release, God had promised to give this motley crew land of their own and make them into a nation. But before He did this, God brought them into the middle of the desert, to a mountain. And there, in the midst of smoke, clouds, fire, thunder, and lightning, God reintroduced Himself to His people. They had heard stories of God's dealings with their forefathers, especially Abraham, Isaac, Jacob, and Joseph. They had heard a lot about God and His promises. But they had been a people of slavery for four hundred years. During this time, access to religious expression had been limited. There were no temples or books, and the people had neglected perpetuating their faith.

So God brought them to this mountain and spoke to them about Himself. "I am the Lord your God, who brought you out of Egypt, out of the land of slavery" (Exodus 20:2). God began with what He had done for them. That's how God is! He always begins with what He has done to show us who He is, while we tend to begin with what we can do for Him. What had God done for them? Everything. Up to that point, the relationship had been one-sided. God took the initiative in sending

Moses to Pharaoh. God coerced the tyrant to liberate the Hebrew slaves. God performed miracles to bring them out of Egypt. God supplied their needs in the desert despite all their complaining. God gave freedom to all who had been slaves. Everything!

But God didn't want a one-sided relationship. Therefore, He began to cast the vision for His people for a new order of life. A life where society would be quite different, even countercultural. He gave His people ten foundational principles for living His way.

WHY NOT THE "TEN SUGGESTIONS"?

When I get something new, I look at it, determine how to use it and how it runs, and then try it out. Only if I find I am not getting it to work will I look at the instructions. When microwaves first came out, in my impatience to cook something quickly, I threw an item into the unit, turned the handle to three minutes, and watched through the little window. The only problem was that sparks were flying everywhere! A small fire started. Why? Because I had left the aluminum foil on. I had not read the clear instructions that warned me not to do this if I wanted to avoid problems. So I turned to the instruction book and learned how to correctly operate the microwave before using it again.

The same thing is true with our lives. God never designed His Top Ten List to be a rigid system of rules so your life would be miserable. His list displayed His character. He knew that we would live life to the fullest and have the most joy if we lived in a way that showed that character in all that we did and thought. God knows how people think, how they respond in different situations, and what they need to have the healthiest relationships with Him and with each other. Therefore, He gave warnings, similar to those in the microwave book. These are healthy rules. When people follow His ways, their lives reflect the fact that they are living their lives well, are following the "Manufacturer's instructions."

Because they reflect the character of God, the Ten Commandments are also the only valid standard of right and holy living. Break the Ten Commandments and judgment falls—and *all* people *do* fail to live by the Ten Commandments at some point in their lives. Only God can keep them perfectly. This is where the Gospel comes in, for when Christ died on the cross He paid on our behalf the penalty we deserved for breaking those laws. This payment can be credited to our ledger if we accept —by faith—Christ's death for us.

Unfortunately, most people see God's list as simply rules, something that indicates only restrictions. That is why they like to do things without God. They try to live life according to the rules they have made up—or by a *lack* of rules—and they fail miserably to find the good life. God's commandments give us a practical framework, a grid to live by. Although on our own we cannot keep them, if we understand their relevance and purpose, and as we ask for God's help, not only will our behavior change, but so will the way we make decisions. God's rules prescribe the foundation upon which human society must be laid if justice, wholeness, and peace are ever to be achieved.

MORE ABOUT
WHY THESE ARE COMMANDS

Let's look at four other reasons for saying that God's Top Ten List is a series of commands and not just a collection of suggestions.

Acceptance of God's Guidance

First, the Ten Commandments help us accept God's guidance. Think of this list as a mirror. When you woke up this morning, you looked in the mirror to examine the damage of the night. A mirror shows reality. As we look into the mirror of God's Word, we find the truth about our lives. And the truth isn't pretty. Jeremiah said it this way: "The heart is deceitful above all things and beyond cure. Who can understand it?" (Jeremiah 17:9). No matter how hard we may try, we cannot correct this problem apart from Christ.

Paul describes the answer to this dilemma in Galatians 3:23–25, "Before this faith came, we were held prisoners by the law, locked up until faith should be revealed. So the law was put in charge to lead us to Christ that we might be justified by faith. Now that faith has come, we are no longer under the supervision of the law." The Law shows us our need for God and leads us to Christ, who alone can give us the power to live righteous lives.

Bridling Sin

Second, the Ten Commandments enable us to bridle sin. I coached my daughter's softball team when she played in high school. Once one of my players had taken a bat, by accident, from the other team. Not until the following week did we find the new bat. Seeing this as not only a coaching moment, but also a teaching opportunity, I asked the team what we should do. I'll never forget some of the answers:

"If they call, we could return it."

"They'll never know it's missing."

"They deserved to lose it if they weren't careful with their equipment."

One unchurched player sat quietly listening to the developing discussion until she couldn't be silent any longer. She simply blurted out, "Doesn't the Bible say, 'Thou shalt not steal'?" Case closed! We returned the bat. God's Top Ten List had again bridled—restrained—the sinful desires of a people and set the standard for living.

Providing Proper Direction

Third, the Ten Commandments help us find the right direction in life. They provide direction in a direction-less world. In some ways the Ten Commandments are like a guidance system for life. They provide a compass in a culture with no bearings. They help keep us headed in the right direction to reach God's best for us.

Usually we accept guidance only from those we trust. That is why it is important for people to get to know God in a personal way, to know His nature, to be aware of His track record in guiding the lives of others. That is why He gave us the Bible, why He told the children of Israel to write down the things He had done for them, to record their history. That history was a record of the sovereign Lord's acts and His nature. In the New Testament we see an even greater picture of who God is and His great love and care for mankind. As a person sees how trustworthy God is, then it becomes easier for him—or her—to respond positively to His guidance, because trust is growing.

Reflecting Personal Passion for God

The Ten Commandments reflect our personal passion for God. How much do you love God? Do you love Him enough to put Him first in your life? Do you love Him enough not to get trapped by idolatry? Do you love Him enough not to misuse His name? Each of these questions is taken from God's Top Ten List, and your answers are a gauge of your personal passion for God. Ultimately, for the unbeliever, it may be this list that drives a person to Christ. Paul said this, as we have already stated: "So the law was put in charge to lead us to Christ that we might be justified by faith" (Galatians 3:24). This list may be a mirror, but it cannot remove the problem it shows us. Only the cleansing blood of Jesus Christ through His redemptive work on the cross can wash away our sin.

CONCLUSION

Probably the most important truth I could tell you as we conclude this chapter is where we can find the fulfillment of God's law. God's Top Ten List has its ultimate expression in the life of Jesus Christ. Paul stated in Galatians 4:4–5, "But when the time had fully come, God sent his Son, born of a woman, born under law, to redeem those under law, that we might receive the full rights of sons."

To examine our Lord's life throughout the Gospels is to see a life in perfect obedience to the Law. Was He one of many? No. He is *the only One* who obeyed perfectly, and so He alone could fulfill all the Old Testament typology seen in Leviticus and Numbers as the spotless Passover Lamb and the Scapegoat.

What can be said of the Law?

- The Law shuts our mouths but opens our eyes.
- The Law condemns but does not convert.
- The Law challenges but does not change.
- The Law points the finger but does not give mercy.

- The Law leaves us without excuse but drives us to Jesus.

- The Law gives us the standard by which we should live our lives.

As you read this book, allow your heart to be drawn to Jesus. God wants what you're about to learn to be written on your heart. Jeremiah, addressing the nation of Israel in the Old Testament, but speaking of a day when Christ would come, said, "'This is the covenant I [God] will make with the house of Israel after that time. . . . I will put my law in their minds and write it on their hearts. I will be their God, and they will be my people'" (Jeremiah 31:33). This very passage was quoted in the New Testament book of Hebrews (see Hebrews 8:9–10, which quotes still more of the passage from Jeremiah). Don't see the pilgrimage you're about to travel as restrictive, but rather as prescriptive, providing guidance for the most exciting way of living you will ever experience —following Christ, and through Him, following God's Top Ten List.

You've been given a certain amount of time to live your life, and you've been asked to make a decision. Are you going to buy into your own game plan, someone else's game plan, or God's game plan? He has told us what is required. And there's only one real choice to make—Jesus Christ—for it is only through a relationship with Him that we can understand and live by God's Top Ten List.

Notes

1. *Merriam Webster's Collegiate Dictionary,* 10th edition, s.v. secularism.
2. Leith Anderson, *Winning the Values War in a Changing Culture* (Minneapolis: Bethany House, 1994), 31.
3. Ravi Zacharias, *Deliver Us from Evil* (Dallas: Word, 1996), 70.

4. George Hunter, *How to Reach Secular People* (Nashville: Abingdon, 1992), 42.
5. Norman Geisler, *Christian Ethics* (Grand Rapids: Baker, 1989), 136.
6. F. LaGard Smith, *When Choice Becomes God* (Eugene, Oreg.: Harvest Pubns., 1990), 10.

chapter two

Keeping Your Priorities Straight

"I am the Lord your God, who brought you out of Egypt, out of the land of slavery. You shall have no other gods before me."

—Exodus 20:2–3

The nineties have not been good to the American language. We have transformed the bathroom plunger into the hydro-force blast cup. Welfare applicants no longer need to meet with clerks, but with eligibility technicians. Bill collectors of the eighties have become the credit analysts of the nineties. Tour guides have the newly developed title of destination adviser, while garbage collectors are now sanitation engineers. Even cemeteries have bought into the changes, advising people of their pre-need arrangements.

But will changes in our vocabulary cause things to get any better? No, tax hikes have become revenue enhancements and have been identified as tax base erosion control devices, but they still cost us money. Deluxe car companies no longer are willing to admit their cars occasionally break down—now they "fail to proceed."

Deaths in battle during the Gulf War became "collateral damage." Can you imagine receiving a telephone call telling you that because your car failed to proceed over the railroad tracks, the train caused some collateral damage to your mate?

Don't be surprised at all the changes. They typify the present condition of our world. This is the climate in which we find ourselves living at the end of the twentieth century. It is now easier to change terminology than to admit failure or acknowledge reality and understand the truth. The bottom line? We have confused our priorities. And when priorities become confused, culture inevitably will find itself in moral crisis, as we have already seen in chapter 1.

When God spoke to Moses in Exodus 20, He was speaking to an entire nation that had lost its priorities. When He gave Israel the Ten Commandments, by design He placed commandment number one exactly where it belongs—first. God was reminding His people, "First things first." He said to Moses, and ultimately to His people, "I am the Lord your God, who brought you out of Egypt, out of the land of slavery. You shall have no other gods before me" (Exodus 20:2–3).

In Moses' day this command would have brought to mind the many specific, named gods worshiped among the nations. Amon-Re (the sun god), Osiris, Isis, Ptah, and Thoth were some of the Egyptian deities. The Baal gods and Asherah and Molech were worshiped among the Canaanites.

Today in the Western world people no longer worship such gods. But that doesn't mean that this command doesn't apply to us. The "other gods" we worship are the things and persons we place before God. God is saying, "I get first place. I want to be number one in your life." Why? Because He is the only true God. He deserves our worship. When we try to worship Him and still give other things priority, we worship two masters. This won't work. Jesus said it this way, "No one can serve two masters" (Matthew 6:24; see Luke 16:13). He didn't say you *shouldn't* serve two masters. He didn't imply, "It's going to be *really tough* to serve two masters." He simply and distinctly stated, "You can't!"

But when our priorities are set with God at the top, it's amazing how everything else falls into place. Don't be surprised. God has already promised this to us. Matthew 6:33 says, "But seek first his kingdom and his righteousness, and all these things will be given to you as well."

Sound easy? No way! This is very difficult to do. The real struggle is not "*Should* I put God first?" The issue is "*How* do I put God first?"

If God wants to be the priority in your life—and He does; and if God does not want any competition from other distractions—and He doesn't, let's look at how we can make God first in all areas of our lives.

OUR FAITH

The key to successfully living the Christian life rests on *where* you place your faith. Scripture states, "According to your faith be it unto you" (Matthew 9:29 KJV). Your faith is going to be put somewhere, either in God or in something or someone else. When problems come, you can focus on them or you can focus on God. The object of your attention, your focus, is where your faith is.

As you get to know God for who He really is and understand His nature and His attributes, your faith and confidence in Him will grow. This is one reason He gives you many opportunities in life for your faith to grow.

Some of these "opportunities" are the hard places in life. But as you experience difficulties you will *choose* whether your faith will grow or be damaged by the way you face them. If you look at God as your source of strength, you will grow, but if you look away from Him and question His nature, His commitment to you, and His love for you, you won't. He wants you to put Him first in your faith, trusting Him and what He has promised you in the Word.

OUR INVOLVEMENT WITH OTHERS

As humans, all of us can get involved in many more things than we have time to accomplish. Some are of value, some not so desirable. That is why God wants us to come to Him, to seek His guidance for the people and things He wants us to get involved with. He knows all about us and all about the future, and so He can direct us to get involved with those things that will be the best for us and for the kingdom.

Have you ever wondered what is greatness in God's eyes? What makes a person great? Well, a great deal of greatness is comparative. When I first moved to Manhattan Beach, I said to some people, "What a great place to live!" And their reply was, "Compared to what?" I was saying that according to my standards, the air was great, the breeze was great, and the freeway system was great. Greatness is often comparative.

For example, if Dave, my worship pastor, says something is great in the area of music, I know he's right because he is an accomplished musician. If Orel Hershiser says that someone is a great pitcher, I would have to take his word on it because of the high standard of excellence he represents. God's view of greatness and our views of greatness may be at opposite poles, but God alone knows what true greatness represents. Therefore, I want to be moving toward His standards, so that when I stand before Him one day, He will be pleased with my efforts. Someone has well said that Abraham Lincoln was not great because he was born in a cabin; he was great because he got out of it. What does it take to get out of our cabin and become great in God's eyes?

Jesus said, "If anyone wants to be first, he must be the very last, and the servant of all" (Mark 9:35). He then painted a word picture showing that true greatness through His eternal lenses includes right involvement in others' lives. "He took a little child and had him stand among them. Taking him in his arms, he said to them, 'Whoever welcomes one of these little children in my name welcomes me; and whoever welcomes me does not welcome me but the one who sent me'" (vv. 9:36–37).

There it is. A key part of true greatness is having time for other people and becoming positively involved in their lives. It's becoming a servant. The world says that greatness and success in life are marked by how much money you make, how new your car is, and how expensive your house is. Jesus says that the vision we must have for our lives is to learn to put people above things. Great people value individuals more than things and are willing to make time for people.

Let's come back to the example of Jesus, who made Himself available to others—to the disciples, to the woman at the well, to Nicodemus. He fed the five thousand, healed the sick, and cast out demons. Wherever He went, He drew a crowd. "But didn't He withdraw to pray by Himself?" Yes, that's where the power comes from in order to be available, caring, involved, and helpful to people. Jesus' entire earthly ministry was a moral example for you and me of what it means to be available to others. This example lasted right up through His death on the cross. We measure our importance by the amount of time and attention we receive. But true greatness is measured by our availability to others and the time we spend with them. This, too, will demonstrate where our priorities lie.

OUR RELATIONSHIPS

God designed humans to have healthy relationships. He showed Adam it was not good for him to be alone. He needed to have a relationship with another person—Eve. Families are designed, in part, to help us develop relationship skills as we learn to interact, hopefully in constructive ways, with our siblings.

Sprinkled through the Scriptures we see healthy relationships developing and maturing over time. One example is Barnabas and Paul. They started out with Barnabas as the stronger of the two; Paul then came to the forefront. Next we see a strain in their relationship because of John Mark, a strain that could well have never been fully restored after they both went their separate ways. However, Paul changed in his relationship with John Mark, finally accepting his value. In Paul's writings we read of the important role John Mark played in Paul's ministry after that reconciliation.

God encourages friendships and positive relationships. But we have to be careful, since every relationship may affect our relationship with the Lord. Not only that, but a healthy relationship can change either for the better or the worse. After twenty-plus years of ministry, I see this as a common area of struggle if God is to have first place in my life. My years of ministry have taught me no longer to be stunned at how easily people are led away from God due to inappropriate relationships. But then, again, Proverbs 12:26 warns us, "A righteous man is cautious in friendship."

This is an area David struggled with. At a time when David should have been out leading his army, putting first things first, doing what God had called him to do, he stayed behind the army and rested in his palace in Jerusalem. One evening, as he strolled on the roof of his palace, he saw Bathsheba bathing—and was tempted to begin an immoral relationship with her. This one wrong relationship affected the rest of his life. He became an adulterer and a murderer, and he never rose to the same spiritual height of usability by God after Bathsheba as he was at before their affair.

Samson struggled with the same character flaw. His question was "How close can I get to the fire without getting burned?" Typically, you don't answer this question without some scars. Samson suffered many of those scars, losing his sight, strength, position and freedom, and finally his life. Why? He failed to keep "first things first" in his relationships. His bad relationships cost him everything. Yes, relationships can make or break a person. That is why the Lord warns, "Bad company corrupts good character" (1 Corinthians 15:33).

I realize that there is tremendous wisdom in learning from personal mistakes, but there is greater wisdom in learning from the mistakes of others. Let's quickly learn this principle, or we will struggle with our priorities.

Joshua applied this principle as he led the people of Israel. After taking over the leadership from Moses and leading the Israelites into the Promised Land—a seemingly impossible task—he issued a challenge to the nation: "If serving the Lord seems undesirable to you, then choose for yourselves this day whom you will serve, whether the gods your forefathers served beyond the

River, or the gods of the Amorites, in whose land you are living. But as for me and my household, we will serve the Lord" (Joshua 24:15).

In other words, you want a godly marriage relationship? Put God first! You desire godly family relationships? Put God first!

Notice the following diagrams:

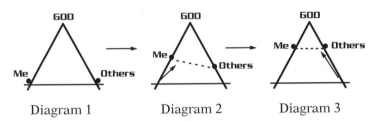

Diagram 1   Diagram 2   Diagram 3

The first diagram shows your relationship to others, with God desiring to be on top. As you grow closer to God, and the "others" in your life just grow a little, the distance between decreases. If both you and your "others" consistently grow in faith, putting first things first, the distance can reduce drastically (the last diagram). This is how commandment number one works. When God is first in your relationships, much (not all) of the conflict is relieved and the tension eased and you grow . . . together.

OUR SPEECH

The tongue. How it can set the world on fire! James 3 gives us an accurate, convicting description of just how dangerous and unruly the tongue can be.

> We put bits into the mouths of horses to make them obey us. . . . Likewise the tongue is a small part of the body, but it makes great boasts. Consider what a great forest is set on fire by a small spark. The tongue also is a fire, a world of evil among the parts of the body. It corrupts the whole

person, sets the whole course of his life on fire, and is itself set on fire by hell. (James 3:3, 5–6)

Just as we put "bits into the mouths of horses to make them obey us," so we need to put "bits" on our tongues in order to exercise control in what we say. Left uncontrolled, the sinful nature of man is to cut others to pieces with the tongue, to use the tongue to manipulate and intimidate others to get one's own way. I must consciously bridle my tongue to make it submit to God's will, not to my old nature. I have to make it a priority to submit my speech to the Lord, to ask Him to control whatever I say, to give me words that help and heal rather than wound and destroy.

This is an ongoing battle and will continue to be a struggle as long as I live in this flesh. How I look forward to the day in heaven when I won't even have a negative thought in my mind, much less be tempted to say those thoughts. It has to be my priority now to "take captive every thought to make it obedient to Christ" (2 Corinthians 10:5). When I put the desire to have His control first in my life, then I am able to have speech that will glorify the Lord.

OUR TRIALS

I can remember being told as a young Christian, "Don't expect all your trials and problems to go away just because you've given your life to Jesus." I heard message after message on James 1:2–4, "Consider it pure joy, my brothers, whenever you face trials of many kinds, because you know that the testing of your faith develops perseverance. Perseverance must finish its work so that you may be mature and complete, not lacking anything."

From 1 Peter 1:6–7 I was told, "In this you greatly rejoice, though now for a little while you may have had to suffer grief in all kinds of trials. These have come so that your faith—of greater worth than gold, which perishes even though refined by fire—may be proved genuine and may result in praise, glory and honor when Jesus Christ is revealed."

"But that's not fair!" I said. "I've given my life to Christ. Why won't He take my trials?" Well, He *will*—but in His own way and timing. We still need to remember the verse "Cast all your anxiety on him because he cares for you" (1 Peter 5:7).

Let me ask you a question. When your next trial hits, to whom will you run for comfort? When you lose a job, burn the turkey, fail the test, have a fight—who is the first one you will run to for help? In speaking for Promise Keepers in 1996, I told pastors and leaders across America, "Prayer is not fourth and punt . . . it's first and ten." Prayer is putting "first things first" by turning to the only One who will always be available to help you through your deepest trials. You'll never get a busy signal when you call on God. You will never have to struggle to get God's attention. The next time a trial strikes (trust me, there will be a next time), don't forget to put God first by praying. In this way you will be keeping your eyes on Him and not on the trial.

OUR PRIORITIES

Our priorities really indicate who we are at the core of our being. What we make time for and what we invest our lives in show where our heart is. Today, time is valued highly. How do you spend your free time? Whatever is your highest priority will probably receive the vast majority of your discretionary time.

What does your planned free time show about you? When do you spend time with the Lord? Is it when your energy level is the highest, or only after you are exhausted from all the other demands of the day and you carve out a little time to read a chapter from the Bible, hoping you do not fall asleep in the process? The Lord makes clear that if we put Him first, make Him our highest priority, then He will not only guide and direct us but will make certain that all we need is supplied (see Proverbs 2:1–5; 3:1–6; Matthew 6:33, among others).

What about your family? Where do they come in your list of priorities? For some people, they are high on the list; for others, mentally they may be high, but in practice other things—such as work and even recreation —are too often allowed to squeeze them out. In fact, we can sometimes be working so hard for someone, or something, that we fail to have any time left for the very one for whom we are investing our time. We need to work so that we can support our family. We need to see our job as a calling, whether or not we work in some kind of Christian ministry. But that doesn't mean we give our families only the scraps of time we have left over.

So this means that even though I am in ministry I have to be careful that I don't let my serving the Lord replace my fellowship with Him. I also have to be careful not to let the many possible demands on my time and service keep me from spending sufficient and proper time with my family. Notice I said *proper.* That means that when one of my sons has a ball game, I make it a point to be there if at all possible. I rearrange my schedule. I place him as the highest priority for that time frame. When my daughter wants me to go to a function at her college, I move heaven and earth to get there. My wife, Nancy, and I have for many years tried to keep the hour between 5:00 P.M. and 6:00 P.M. free so we can attempt to have dinner as a family. We take several walks together each week, to talk and keep our marriage fresh and exciting. Let me tell you, it is not always easy to work these priorities into our schedules, but it is very rewarding. These are precious times to us even after twenty-four years of marriage. We both look forward to these times alone. It is a "first things first" priority.

OUR LEISURE PURSUITS

What do you like to do for fun? What's your hobby? What kind of activities do you include in your recreation time? You can tell a lot about me by simply looking at what I get really excited about. I love to coach. I have coached my daughter's softball and soccer teams and my two sons' baseball, soccer, and roller hockey teams. Why? Because it's fun and I get to spend time with my kids. But I also realize I can still maintain "first things first" in my coaching.

Sometimes my pursuit of "first things" gets expressed in unorthodox ways. I'm as strong a believer as any that the pulpit is sacred and the proclamation of God's message a serious and solemn responsibility. But there have been times when I've stretched the envelope, as the saying goes, as a way of reaching out.

A few years back, some of my softball players at Redondo Union High School were having some difficulty remembering the softball "signs" (you know—steal, take, bunt). So I told them that at church that week I was going to use those signs during my message. At the next practice, I'd buy a soda for anyone who could catch all the signs. Girls who had never attended church in their lives sat intently focused on my every word and move as I spoke from God's Word. To the average member of my church, some of my movements during the sermon might have appeared a little "different." But to those softball players I was speaking directly to them and conveying the idea that something they considered important was also important to me—and even to God. That year two girls on the team came to Christ. Why? God was included in my leisure time. Paul told us in 1 Corinthians 10:31, "So whether you eat or drink or whatever you do, do it all for the glory of God." Whatever I do? Absolutely. That's putting first things first.

OUR ABILITIES

Our abilities may be many or few. But they are *all* given to us by the Lord. He has a wonderful plan for our lives, and this includes the right use of our abilities. Therefore, we need to recognize that we are to exercise them to fulfill His will, His plans for our lives, and not go off in our own, self-centered way. Unfortunately, the talented believer can get off-base with God by wanting to use his talents to fulfill his own desires, rather than seeking God's input.

The greater our abilities, the more vulnerable we are to seeing ourselves as independent of God. That's because our great abilities make us think we're too skillful to need to depend on Him. Yet the opposite is actually true. The greater our abilities, the more we need to recognize that they come from Him—and make certain *He* gets all the glory, not us. As part of this, we need to make certain we are trusting the Lord as we exercise our abilities and are not allowing our abilities to make us independent of Him. When we put our abilities into His hands, we will find that this brings us the most satisfaction. That is the only way to "put first things first" when it comes to our abilities.

OUR MONEY

Few things in life cause a mix-up in priorities more than how we deal with our money. There are more than two thousand references to money in the Scriptures, and yet I wonder how many Christians are dominated by the world's attitude toward money rather than God's. As with abilities, money can become a stronghold in our lives and cause us to get off balance. So, if "first things" are to become a priority, a critical look at our check-books is a must.

We are only managers in the first place. God said in Exodus 19:5, "The whole earth is mine." The whole earth is *whose?* God's. This being true, I am given the privilege of handling someone else's resources, and every entry in my checkbook becomes a spiritual decision of priorities. If God owns it all, I must hold in an open hand everything He has entrusted to me, for I should not cling to that which I do not own.

"We live in a culture of acquisitions," my friend Glenn Wagner once told me. How true. God even warns us about this reality. Proverbs 23:4–5 says, "Do not wear yourself out to get rich; have the wisdom to show re-straint. Cast but a glance at riches, and they are gone, for they will surely sprout wings and fly off to the sky like an eagle." So, if you give firstfruits of your grain, you get . . . ? That's right . . . more grain. This is the prin-ciple of sowing and reaping. (See Galatians 6:7.) God tells me to put my money where my faith is.

OUR EXAMPLE

I used to think Paul was a conceited person because he said in several places that he wanted his readers to imitate him or follow his example (1 Corinthians 4:16;

11:1; Philippians 3:17). *How arrogant,* I thought! No! Rather, how well he knew that his life was being lived in the way Jesus would live it, and therefore he could safely tell his readers that they should follow his example.

But I can hear you thinking, *Well, that's all right for Paul to say. After all, he was an apostle; he was mentored by Jesus. I am not.* Friends, we are *all* to do the same. Like it or not, your life is an example to others—either a good one or a bad one, but nonetheless, an example.

And Jesus is *our* example.

When you find time to be with your children and give them encouragement and love, you model what it is to be a good father. When you find time to study the Bible and to pray, you are a model for your children of what it takes "behind the scenes" to live the Christian life. When you deal with people at work in an honest, ethical way, you model for them and for your family what it means to let your faith affect your daily decisions. In Ephesians 4:1–3 Paul urges us "to live a life worthy of the calling you have received. Be completely humble and gentle; be patient, bearing with one another in love. Make every effort to keep the unity of the Spirit through the bond of peace." Do you do these things?

Because I am a believer, God expects me to reflect His life and His value system. God wants me to be a positive example to believers and nonbelievers alike of the difference God's life makes flowing through people. The world is full of pride. I am to be completely humble. The world strives to get its own way. I am to be gentle and patient and loving, operating in a peaceful way. This will only happen when I allow His Spirit to control my life— when I put Him first in my responses.

Truly I have to put first things first in my life in order to fulfill this overwhelming standard God sets for my life. When He is first, when I am Spirit-controlled, then I am in a right position and am a good example of His life flowing through me, no matter how the world may think I should act. And believe me, they will notice, and they will usually be amazed by the one who lives a Spirit-filled life before them and sets an example they wish they could match.

CONCLUSION

The story is told of a young man from the South who visited a friend in Wyoming in the middle of the winter. One afternoon when the temperature was five degrees below zero, the two took a drive in the country. Seeing a frozen lake, they parked the car and decided to explore. The Wyoming native immediately headed toward the center of the frozen lake. The man from the South adopted a more conservative strategy. He decided to explore around the edge of the lake, never venturing more than six feet from shore. To be extra cautious, he even walked on his tiptoes, attempting to create as little pressure on the ice as possible. Suddenly, he heard a loud roar. Turning his head, he saw a local farmer driving a huge tractor across the middle of the ice. He took a moment to look down at his feet as he was standing on his tiptoes and couldn't help but laugh at the contrast. The farmer on the tractor—he on his tiptoes. What was the difference? The local farmer knew the ice. He trusted the foundation he was driving across. The visitor, on the other hand, did not know a lot about frozen lakes and therefore did not trust the foundation.[1]

A lot of Christians are fearfully tiptoeing around the edge of their relationship with God simply because they do not know and have failed to comprehend just how trustworthy He is. There is no need to tiptoe around

God. His faithfulness will support you. Just give Him first place in your life.

Note

1. Adapted from "Faith Planning," by Bruce Cook, p. 112, as quoted in *Parables* (January 1990): 7.

chapter three

The Benefits of Worshiping the True God

"You shall not make for yourself an idol in the form of anything in heaven above or on the earth beneath or in the waters below. You shall not bow down to them or worship them; for I, the Lord your God, am a jealous God, punishing the children for the sin of the fathers to the third and fourth generation of those who hate me, but showing love to a thousand generations of those who love me and keep my commandments."

—Exodus 20:4–6

The announcement was made in 1996 with much agony and regret. The Cleveland Browns NFL football team was moving to Baltimore, Maryland, after thirty years in Cleveland. Among the many Browns' fans interviewed, one man sat in his pickup truck and wept as he told his feelings concerning the loss of the esteemed football team to another city: "Now me and my family will have no place to go on Sunday."

The saddest commentary on this man's words is the realization that his worship at the football shrine in Cleveland can be seen all across America. People may not understand the significance or relationship between the Old Testament and the New Testament. People cannot identify the four Gospels, the Law, or even significant truths other generations have taken for granted. But they can certainly tell you the starting fullback for the Cowboys, the best pitcher for the Dodgers, and the big game of the week to be aired this weekend. All because of the idolatry of modern-day athletes and programs.

However, it is not just at the professional level we see such sports idolatry. Ask any pastor of a town with a successful sports program if he avoids scheduling important events at game times. Even ministries in a sophisticated, large area such as Southern California can too often run into conflict with sporting events. For example, church attendance is always down on the West Coast when the World Series or the Super Bowl starts anytime on Sunday morning. Sadly, God too often loses out in the battle for our hearts when the Enemy's weapon is sports.

UNDERSTANDING HISTORY

How can we know when we have switched from worshiping the true God to worshiping a substitute? We can know by applying the second commandment to our pursuits and priorities. This commandment must be a very important one for God to use so many words in stating it. Knowing the heart of man and how he tries to get around laws, God did not want there to be any wiggle room or any way for someone to say, "I didn't understand."

"You shall not make for yourself an idol in the form of anything in heaven above or on the earth beneath or in the waters below. You shall not bow down to them or worship them; for I, the Lord your God, am a jealous God, punishing the children for the sin of the fathers to the third and fourth generation of those who hate me, but showing love to a thousand generations of those who love me and keep my commandments." (Exodus 20:4–6)

This second command was closely allied to the first: "You shall have no other gods before me" (Exodus 20:3). God was teaching the Israelites important lessons about who He is and how He works. God wanted to be clear and firm. No images! No exceptions!

Back in the times in which God gave His Top Ten List, idolatry was blatant. This idolatry involved "gods" made from wood and stone and usually covered with some precious metal. Throughout the Bible, we read of many who made their living from idols. Terah, Abraham's father, worshiped other gods (Joshua 24:2), and Rachel stole the household gods owned by her father Laban (Genesis 31:19–37).

When Moses was delayed on Mount Sinai "[the people] gathered around Aaron and said, 'Come, make us gods who will go before us'" (Exodus 32:1), asking for a visible, handmade idol. When Aaron responded by fashioning a calf from gold donated by the people they said, "These are your gods, O Israel, who brought you up out of Egypt" (v. 4). *The Illustrated Bible Dictionary* says of this incident,

The whole narrative of the golden calf (Exodus 32) reveals the extent of the contrast between the religion which stemmed from Mt. Sinai and the form of religion congenial to the unregenerated heart. These religions, we learn, are incompatible . . . they corrupt themselves with images. This is the essential Mosaic position, as recorded in the Decalogue.[1]

In Leviticus the Lord said, "Do not turn to idols or make gods of cast metal for yourselves. I am the Lord your God" (Leviticus 19:4). Yet repeatedly the people turned to idols, although when good kings reigned they tore down the idols and the worship sites devoted to them.

King Ahab "behaved in the vilest manner by going after idols, like the Amorites the Lord drove out before Israel" (1 Kings 21:26). King Manasseh "led Judah into sin with his idols" (2 Kings 21:11). The Israelites "worshiped other gods and followed the practices of the nations the Lord had driven out before them. . . . They set up sacred stones and Asherah poles on every high hill and under every spreading tree. . . . They worshiped idols, though the Lord had said, 'You shall not do this.'" (2 Kings 17:7–8, 10, 12).

A good king, Josiah, "got rid of the mediums and spiritists, the household gods, the idols and all the other detestable things seen in Judah and Jerusalem. . . . Neither before nor after Josiah was there a king like him who turned to the Lord as he did" (2 Kings 23:24–25). Josiah tore down the "the altars of the Baals . . . ; he cut to pieces the incense altars that were above them, and smashed the Asherah poles, the idols and the images" (2 Chronicles 34:4). So also King Asa, who "removed the detestable idols from the whole land of Judah and Benjamin and . . . repaired the altar of the Lord that was in front of the portico of the Lord's temple" (2 Chronicles 15:8).

The prophets condemned idol worship, and we know from the biblical record that idol worship was one of the reasons God let the Israelites be led into captivity by their enemies. "Your altars will be demolished and your incense altars will be smashed; and I will slay your people in front of your idols" (Ezekiel 6:4). "This is what the Sovereign Lord says: When any Israelite sets up idols in his heart and puts a wicked stumbling block before his face . . . I the Lord will answer him myself in keeping with his great idolatry. . . . Repent! Turn from your idols and renounce all your detestable practices!" (Ezekiel 14:4, 6).

OUR IDOLS

What about us? Most people in the Western world do not worship actual objects. But that doesn't mean we don't worship idols. Entertainment and sports can sometimes push the worship of God off the schedule. The disappointed Browns' fan who said, "Now me and my family will have no place to go on Sunday" revealed where his idols lay. Super Bowl Sunday and World Series games and football stadiums can be shrines. Increasingly in our culture today, people are worshiping their own gods. Some drive their gods to and from work. Others live in their gods. A few look in the mirror and idolize their god of looks.

The New Age tells us that we are all gods and only have to discover the "godness" in us and let it come out. Is it any wonder, then, that we are constantly tempted to self-indulgence and, in essence, self-worship? "You're worth it, baby" and "I'll do it my way" are the mantras of this New Age thinking, as well as of less sophisticated human-centered religions. Unfortunately, we are living in an age in which people have forgotten the benefits of worshiping the true God and thus end up reducing God to the size and demeanor they desire. After all, people in America live for choices. John Hammond and James Morrison say in *The Stuff Americans Are Made Of:*

Choice is the First Force in America. It is formative and formidable. Overwhelming at times. We can't escape the power of choice in dealing with money markets, consumer preference, fashion fads, public policy, or rebellious teenagers who won't pick up their rooms. Our Constitution, the oldest written constitution in the world, guarantees each American choice in speech, choice in what is written, choice of religion, choice in association, choice even in choosing or not choosing a weapon. Finally, and most important, there is choice in how we are governed, and by whom.[2]

And choice has become a powerful force even when it comes to our own personal governing, our spiritual governing.

But we're fooling ourselves if we think we can control our own lives. One little girl had it right when she prayed, "Please Lord, take care of Dad and Mom and Bobby and Aunt Kitty and be sure to take care of Yourself, or else we're all sunk." Her understanding of God's power was childish but she recognized better than many adults how much we need God.

If America has many other options to God, does that mean God is ignored? What may surprise you is the fact that many Americans strongly believe there is a true God. In George Barna's landmark study, *What Americans Believe,* he reported the results he got when he asked people how much they agreed with the concept "There is a God who is holy and perfect, who created the world and rules it today." Seventy-four percent strongly agreed; 12 percent agreed somewhat; 8 percent disagreed strongly, 5 percent disagreed somewhat; and 3 percent didn't know.[3]

Three years later, in the book *Virtual America,* Barna posed the question in a slightly different way and got some interesting answers. He asked people to tell him what beliefs they had about God. Sixty-seven percent believed that God was an "all-powerful, all-knowing Creator who rules the world today." Thirty-three percent were divided among several more skeptical views: 2 percent thought "there is no such thing as God"; 3 percent that "there are many gods, each different"; 3 percent that "everyone is God"; 8 percent that God represents "total realization of personal, human potential"; 10 percent held that God is a "state of higher consciousness a person may reach"; and 7 percent didn't know what God was like.[4]

GOD-SUBSTITUTES

We are spiritual beings, made for a relationship with God. So this second piece of God's Top Ten puzzle is not necessarily about shrines in our living room, although some are guilty of this. It's more about understanding what or who is at the center of our hearts. What do you grab onto to fill that "hole in your soul" and meet your spiritual needs of legitimacy and meaning? Whatever you answered has become your God-substitute. That is idolatry. Remember what the apostle Paul said to the Ephesians?

> But among you there must not be even a hint of sexual immorality, or of any kind of impurity, or of greed, because these are improper for God's holy people. . . . For of this you can be sure: No immoral, impure or greedy person—such a man is an idolater—has any inheritance in the kingdom of Christ and of God. (Ephesians 5:3, 5)

This broadens our definition of idolatry, doesn't it? Paul was stern about idolatry because he saw that these believers were a people tempted to put someone or something else in God's spot.

They had the lure of Zeus and Baal. The Pantheon was a temple in Rome dedicated to all the gods. Those false gods are certainly not very tempting to the modern mind, are they? Today there's a new Pantheon in town, and it includes the gods Paul alluded to in the passage quoted above. This Pantheon contains myriad things that consume our lives, our allegiance, and our devotion. Each may be a good thing in its place but can easily become a substitute for God.

Money and Possessions

Some God-substitutes come in the form of money and possessions. They become our status symbols and source of ultimate security. But it doesn't take long before you discover just how much these things disappoint. A couple of years ago I bought my oldest son, Scott, a telescope from a television shopping channel. I heard the guy on TV rant and rave about its capabilities. I was trying to figure out how in the world I could fit this twenty-dollar telescope into Scott's room. It looked so large on the television. But when it came in the mail, it didn't take two movers to cart the telescope to the door. It was not the product I thought it was. "Stuff" just seems to let you down and can never substitute for the true God.

Work and Status

Some God-substitutes come in the form of work and status, especially for men, because work tends to become their main source of fulfillment. Now, don't get me wrong, hard work is good and right. Yet work-centered people easily become workaholics. This is a god that can seem so right—the need to be a good provider for our family and to give them the things they need and desire.

But just as we can easily get our eyes off Jesus in our leisure pursuits, we can focus so much on the process of work that we get our eyes off the ones for whom we are working those long hours. Work is to glorify God and to provide for those we love. It is not just to acquire material goods and give us an excuse for ignoring our families. When those things happen, work has replaced the position of our families and even God.

How can you tell when you've put yourself ahead of God in your priorities? Well, one good rule of thumb is to evaluate how willing you are to sacrifice for work the time you really should spend with the Lord or with your family. This can be more subtle than just missing important events or special family observances. For example, you're sitting at the dinner table wishing everyone would hurry up so you can get back to work. Such behavior is the reason we have coined the statement, "He's here, but 'nobody's at home.'"

Another indication is when you find yourself often making excuses or apologizing for missing something important because your work interfered. Listen! This is not God's standard. He should be our priority. Within that priority we need to have a good balance in our lives between work, family, and leisure. Ask Him to show you how to do that in your current situation.

The desire for status is an ego-thing. Such desires can become the driving force in our lives, supplanting anything that challenges the achievement of further status. Too often, again, it is family and God that get knocked out of the way of the one who is seeking more status.

Spouse and Family

Some God-substitutes come in the form of spouse and family. These are the relationships in life that are the most intimate and growth-producing. It may seem appropriate at first glance to think these relationships should be in this central place. But evidence shows differently. We find people who become codependent on other people. Others, in search of the "Brady Bunch" or "Cosby" families, become disillusioned and bitter. Each family mix is unique. When God is the center, He will help your family reach its full potential. Again, a God-perspective on what your family should be is essential to live the full, abundant life God offers each of His children.

Personal Selfishness

The most familiar God-substitute today is personal selfishness. My wants, my needs always come first. When opportunity knocks, my initial question becomes, "What's in it for me?" Such self-centered thoughts are destructive to our relationships with others, including our family, as well as our relationship with the Lord.

MAKING CHOICES

Are there other God-substitutes? You bet! You could probably create a list as long as I can. Knowledge, pleasure, power, sex, friends, enemies, anything! Soon our priorities are all affected. Our decisions revolve around our "god." Let's say you have just been offered a major promotion at work. This promotion involves a decent pay raise, but it will require a significant increase in work hours. People who work in this position all put in at least seventy hours, and you will certainly be expected to do the same.

If your "god" is money and possessions, this is a no-brainer. More bucks means more stuff. You hope your family will understand and appreciate the sacrifice you are making in order to provide for them.

If your "god" is work and status, again, easy decision. This new position will bring advancement, recognition, and fulfillment. Your family and friends should be proud of you. Besides, if you are making sacrifices, they should be ready to do the same.

If your "god" is your spouse and family, the decision becomes a little tougher. You want to please your spouse, so what you decide might depend upon the kind of picture you desire to paint. Do you want a family where you are home every night, playing catch with the kids and chasing the dog in the yard? Or do you want a really nice home and a large yard with a built-in pool? If the picture is the latter, the choice is an easy one.

What if my "god" is me? Then I will probably do what does the most good for myself. I will focus on my needs and wants. I will seek my own self-fulfillment. I will seek to satisfy my innermost desires.

Can you see how this works? But when I put God at the center of my life, I will focus on the big picture. What does He want me to become? Can I make a significant contribution to the cause of Christ in making this change? Will I grow in my faith? Will this new position enhance my relationships with the people God has placed in my life? The entire grid for decision making changes.

We can see the whole of our life as a Polaroid picture. God has a snapshot of the "you" He wants and is in the process of developing. There are no "negatives." Instead, the picture develops as we live our lives. Be patient. With Him at the center, life becomes an exciting process of experiencing the varied colors of life He intended. Life continues to have splotches of boredom, loneliness, and pain. And, yes, life doesn't someday "become" meaningful or interesting. It is interesting now. It is leading somewhere, and God needs to be at the center of our lives.

WHAT GOD IS REALLY LIKE

What are some of God's attributes? I have provided a chart to help you look through these attributes in a clear and precise way. To examine this chart is to recognize the greatness and the majesty of our Creator. So many times we focus in on and exaggerate the things we fear. Sometimes this fear is exhibited as worry. Simultaneously we eliminate our focus upon God. May I suggest you emphasize the greatness of God, praise Him, and allow Him to work on those areas of fear. The chart on page 61 is a list of some of the many ways the Bible describes God.

If you really want to know God, why not take one or two characteristics each day, look up the verses in the Bible, and then meditate on what that trait means to you. This will revolutionize your conception of God. Suddenly you will understand why God doesn't like substitutes for Himself. Nothing can compare with Him. The substitutes will always fall short. He alone is worthy of worship, and following any other "god" always leads to trouble. This is why God says, "You shall not bow down to them or worship them; for I, the Lord your God, am a jealous God, punishing the children for the sin of the fathers to the third and fourth generation of those who hate me, but showing love to a thousand generations of those who love me and keep my commandments" (Exodus 20:5–6).

MORE ABOUT WHY GOD
DOESN'T LIKE IMAGES OF HIMSELF

Have you ever wondered why God is so emphatic about this issue? "Come on, God—what's the big deal about a little statue or my love for my car? I still love

God Is . . .	Meaning	References
Triune	Three "persons" unified into one God	Deuteronomy 6:4; Matthew 28:19; Acts 5:30–32; Philippians 2:6–11
Infinite	Unlimited and unlimitable	1 Kings 8:27; Acts 17:24
Eternal	Free from the succession of time	Genesis 21:33; Psalm 90:2
Immutable	Unchanging and unchangeable	James 1:17
Sovereign	Supreme ruler	Exodus 23:17
Omnipresent	Everywhere at all times (not *in* everything)	Psalm 139:7–12
Omniscient	Knows all actual and possible things	Psalm 33:13–15; Hebrews 4:13
Omnipotent	All-powerful	Genesis 17:1; Matthew 19:26
Just	Moral equity (no respect of persons)	Acts 17:31
Love	Seeks the highest good	Ephesians 2:4–5; 1 John 4:10
Truth	Honest and consistent with Himself	John 14:6
Independent	Doesn't need anyone nor anything	Isaiah 40:13; Romans 11:33–36
Holy	Righteous or pure	Job 34:12; 1 John 1:5

You. I'm just excited about this other stuff too!" Why does God want us not to make any images *at all* of what we think is "god"?

Images Are Inadequate

One reason is that no image is adequate. Each image that might have been used to represent God would cause its own misunderstandings. The young bull Aaron used as his model for "god" represented strength, but also virility and sexual prowess. As a created animal it could not represent God's complete holiness, power, and knowledge. The human forms people used as idols also imputed human weaknesses. Man was created in God's image, but that didn't mean that God is like man, because God is infinite. God is the Creator; every time we try to equate Him to a creature, we limit Him.

A famous analogy helps to explain. Imagine three people who have been blindfolded and given the responsibility of describing an elephant. Each person could comprehend it only as he experienced it, but none would be able to comprehend the whole. The one who stood at the elephant's side might describe it as a monstrous animal with four enormous legs. The second would sense it was a weird-shaped tubular animal with unusual height as he stood facing the elephant's trunk. The third . . . well, you get the idea. Each has his own experience. But none has the complete picture. Likewise, there are no statues, no images, no drawings capable of declaring the greatness of the Almighty. We have trouble following this premise, just as the people of Israel did. John I. Durham writes, "The amount of attention given to the second commandment . . . shows that it . . . was a difficult one for the people of Israel to keep."[5]

Images Are Localized

A second reason for God's disgust with images is that we might think God is localized. Even Israel later believed that God resided in the ark of the covenant or the temple. An image would have been even worse. They would have believed that God resided in the image, and then come to view the image as God. But God is omnipresent; He's everywhere, all the time.

A great example of this imagery on the big screen occurred in the now-famous *Raiders of the Lost Ark.* Those seeking to discover the ark's whereabouts looked for the power in the creation rather than the Creator. The same concept can be identified in *Indiana Jones and the Last Crusade,* where the cup contained the "power."

Images Give the Delusion of Control

A third reason for God to be so against idols is that when we have made them we might think that means we can control God. In cultures that worship images, the image itself not only is believed to be the home of the god, but eventually is believed to have divine powers. Thus, were one to possess an image of the one true God or even a piece of it, man might try to manipulate God—but God is independent.

As much as God tried to avoid this pitfall for the Israelites, they still leaned toward seeing God as indwelling the items He had given them that were part of the temple. For example, in 1 Samuel 4:3 we read of the Israelites' doing battle with the Philistines and losing. The Israelites were confused and responded, "Why did the Lord bring defeat upon us today before the Philistines? Let us bring the ark of the Lord's covenant from Shiloh, so that it may go with us and save us from the hand of our enemies." *Who* was to save them? The Lord Jehovah? No, they said the presence of the ark would do the trick. Did it? At first the Philistines trembled in fear saying, "A god has come into the camp. . . . We're in trouble! Nothing like this has happened before. Woe to us! Who will deliver us from the hand of these mighty gods?" (vv. 7–8). But the Philistine leaders rallied their troops and fought back courageously and victoriously, slaughtering thirty thousand Jews—and capturing the ark itself. So much for God and the ark of the covenant being synonymous!

Yes, God knows human nature. We are no different today. Many people carry a rabbit's foot around for luck. (But how lucky was the rabbit that lost his foot so a person could have a charm?) Or how about those groups that have a statue for various problems one can face that are meant to ward off that kind of trouble in the owner's life?

God Is Spirit

At Sinai, God gave yet another reason for not making images when He pointed out to the Israelites that they saw no shape or form, but only heard His voice: "You have seen for yourselves that I have spoken to you from heaven" (Exodus 20:22). God did not allow the Israelites to approach Him on the mountain (19:10–12, 20–23; 20:18–23) but spoke to Moses on Mount Sinai through thick clouds and smoke (19:16–25).

Later Moses asked to see God: "Show me your glory" (33:18). God replied,

> "I will cause all my goodness to pass in front of you, and I will proclaim my name, the Lord, in your presence. . . . But . . . you cannot see my face, for no one may see me and live. . . . There is a place near me where you may

stand on a rock. When my glory passes by, I will put you in a cleft in the rock and cover you with my hand until I have passed by. Then I will remove my hand and you will see my back; but my face must not be seen." (vv. 19–23)

In the New Testament, when Jesus gave a description of God He said that He has no body but rather "is spirit" (John 4:24). Thus, to give Him a form would be to give a wrong, distorted view of who God truly is. He is unlimited. Not even the grand temple Solomon built could contain Him.

This is reinforced in John 1:18, "No one has ever seen God." And this includes Moses, who saw His glory but was not allowed to see more lest he die. Yet just being in His presence, without actually "seeing" God, caused his face to shine so much that it had to be covered with a veil so that the people could bear looking at him (Exodus 34:29–35). Pretty powerful stuff, I'd say.

The closest we come to seeing God is to see Jesus. That is why Jesus says to Philip in John 14:9, "Don't you know me, Philip, even after I have been among you such a long time? Anyone who has seen me has seen the Father."

Images Are Not the Original

Sadly, we as humans have a tendency to worship what is on the "outside," images, even though God has told us not to do this. This comes with our fallen nature. Our nature wants to do things its way and does not want to be told whom or what to worship. Oh, yes, we are willing to worship, but our fallen nature wants to do it on its terms and to maintain, therefore, a degree of control. When we worship images of any type, we lose sight of the thing that the image represents. We begin to think that the image itself has power and personality. Could this be why no one has found the ark of the covenant? The cup from the Last Supper? Noah's ark?

God Has Exclusive Right to Our Lives

God really means business on this commandment, as He does with all of them. But He gets especially pointed when He says in Exodus 20:5, "For I, the Lord your God, am a jealous God, punishing the children for the sin of the fathers to the third and fourth generation of those who hate me." The word *jealous* can also be translated "zealous." It's not a negative term as we tend to view it today. It refers more to an "action" than an "emotion." It's not a statement of intolerance so much as it is a statement of exclusiveness. God sees His relationship with us to be like that of a marriage. No loving husband would share his wife with someone else.

The statement declaring punishment to the third and fourth generations is not a math problem. (If Johnny worships another god when he is twelve years old, how old would he be when God stops punishing his family?) Rather, it is more a statement of who God is and how He operates. We can't say that all suffering is punishment for sin, but we *do* know that consequences follow disobedience to God. Note who is punished: "Those who hate me"; in other words, those who refuse to live their lives according to God's will.

In the next verse God provides a promise, a covenant: "Showing love to a thousand generations of those who love me and keep my commandments" (v. 6). God's love is tremendous. The emphasis of the last two verses lands primarily here. In other words, God will punish those who hate Him, but more importantly He will show love to those who love Him. Previously He listed four generations, but here He refers to a thousand generations. Please notice the connection between loving God and keeping His commandments. In God's eyes, there is no difference. Love is a decision, not a feeling.

You see, it's not about idols on my mantel, it's about understanding and honoring the vastness of God.

THE BENEFITS OF WORSHIPING GOD

In Genesis 1:27, the Bible says, "So God created man in his own image, in the image of God he created him; male and female he created them." Today, many attempt to do the opposite and make God in their own image. Psalm 118:24 says, "This is the day the Lord has made; let us rejoice and be glad in it." Today people want that verse to read, "This is the Lord the day has made." Every day there are new "images" of God being created. Because they are powerless gods, they never truly satisfy their creators. What a contrast when one finally discovers the real Lord of Lords and King of Kings and experiences the tremendous benefits of this wonderful relationship. Here are three benefits you must never forget.

Fulfillment

First, to worship the true God means fulfillment. If you give your life totally to Jesus Christ, you will experience a fulfillment that can never be experienced any other way. You may search for all the other substitutes, but with great clarity and precision the Bible declares, "But seek first his kingdom and his righteousness, and all these things will be given to you as well" (Matthew 6:33). Do you know how fulfilling life becomes when you have a sense of security? The Lord Jesus Christ is the only One who can claim that He will never leave you or forsake you, and He will follow through on that promise.

Freedom

Second, to worship the true God means freedom. We do not need to be dominated by things. There is no freedom when life is a constant search for more. Real freedom is only found in Christ. Some of the Jewish people to whom our Lord was ministering finally grasped this truth when they heard, "If you hold to my teaching, you are really my disciples. Then you will know the truth, and the truth will set you free" (John 8:31–32).

From what do you need freedom today? Have you been carrying around guilt that has paralyzed you for years? Jesus will free you! Has an addiction so tortured you that you have no hope? Let Jesus free you! Are you lonely? Has life been a random series of disappointments? Jesus is waiting for you to seek His freedom!

A Future

Third, to worship the true God means to have a future. "Things" in general don't last. Only two, apart from God, last forever: God's Word and people. To worship the true God, the Lord Jesus, is to live forever in His presence. Because God is spirit—and we are not born with a spirit that is alive—if we are ever to live eternally with Him we must have His Spirit in us bringing our spirit to life. This is why Jesus came and why we need to be born again. If we come to the end of our lives and are still spiritually dead, then it will be impossible for us to spend eternity with God, who is spirit. We can only spend it in the place of those who are spiritually dead— hell. Strong words, yes, but biblically sound. John 3:16 tells us, "For God so loved the world that he gave his one and only Son, that whoever believes in him shall not perish but have eternal life."

CONCLUSION

What is the shape of your god today? Could you be missing out on the blessings of worshiping the true God? When I was a teenager, my god had a home plate and a home-run fence. I went to college where I discovered a new god, which was handed to me at a commencement ceremony. It was then off to the next phase of life and idolatry, where my god became popularity. I was a teacher and coach who was always winning or in charge of something. I even had a yearbook dedicated to me. You know what—that "stuff" doesn't last very long. They faded away just as quickly as they were received. But Jesus Christ has set me free. I've learned to allow Him to be the hub of my life, and the ride is so much smoother.

Be careful how you live. The Bible says in 1 John 5:21, "Dear children, keep yourselves from idols." That will mean daily decisions, daily choices. But remember, every choice you make has a consequence. Worshiping God requires your complete surrender and devotion. The prize is eternal life beginning the moment you believe. No-brainer, huh?

Notes

1. *The Illustrated Bible Dictionary* (Leicester, England: Inter-Varsity, 1980; pub. and distrib. in the United States and Canada by Tyndale, Wheaton, Ill.), 2:678.
2. John Hammond and James Morrison, *The Stuff Americans Are Made Of* (New York: Macmillan, 1996), 34.
3. George Barna, *What Americans Believe* (Ventura, Calif.: Regal, 1991), 201.
4. George Barna, *Virtual America* (Ventura, Calif.: Regal, 1994), 110.
5. John I. Durham, *Exodus,* Word Biblical Commentary, vol. 3 (Waco, Tex.: Word, 1987), 3:286.

chapter four

It's All in a Name

"You shall not misuse the name of the Lord your God, for the Lord will not hold anyone guiltless who misuses his name."
—Exodus 20:7

What's in a name? A lot more than we think. Names mean a great deal. They help create initial impressions. A recent NBC *Dateline* program discussed the efforts Hollywood goes through to name a movie. High-powered marketing companies use focus groups to determine this information.

When my wife and I gave our children their names, we prayed long and hard about the right name, knowing that in Bible times a person's name represented a lifetime of character traits and values. Names are important. A friend told me a story about his nephew, a five-year-old named Andrew. Andrew was on an airplane flight recently, when he was upgraded to first class and separated from his mother. (Hard to believe, but this actually happened.) The ticket and seat assignment said "Stockman," Andrew's last name. The stewardess approached him and asked, "Mr. Stockman, what do I call you?" "Mr. Stockman will be fine." So, for the rest of the flight . . . "Mr. Stockman, may I adjust your seat for you?" "Mr. Stockman, would you like some more juice?" "Mr. Stockman, would you like me to cut your meat for you?" Young Andrew wanted to be treated with respect. And even at his tender age, he knew that respect for his name meant respect for him as a person.

Our names are more than just words that people use to get our attention. A person's name refers to the person himself and brings up the essence and character of that person. Look at the following list.

> Abraham Lincoln
> Martin Luther King Jr.
> John F. Kennedy
> Lee Harvey Oswald
> Mother Teresa
> Adolf Hitler
> John Calvin

What came to mind as you read those names? Wasn't it the specific individuals and what they stood for? You thought of their nature and character in a brief instant. Some names were better to read than others. A person's name refers to the actual person. And how we treat a person's name reflects how we view that person. Thus, as God brought the people of Israel out of Egypt and gathered them at the foot of the mountain, where He reintroduced Himself to them, He cast a vision for a new society, an alternative community, giving them Ten Principles for Living. The Third Commandment represents a principle that was essential as to how they would interact with God in this new relationship with Him.

I have been fascinated by the way God has so many

names for Himself. You and I usually have a first name (which may be compounded), a middle name, and our family name. Some cultures even add a mother's maiden name to the last name. Royalty often has a multitude of names (eight or more can be strung together for the middle names). But these names do not usually have anything special to do with what we are like. But God's names are different. Each name reveals another aspect of His nature. And God's nature is so complex that it takes a great number of names for Him to reveal to us many of the qualities He possesses.

If you look at the Old Testament, you will find God progressively revealing more and more about Himself to humanity through His names. It is like looking through a small peephole at a construction sight. You have a very limited view at first. But as the hole is enlarged, you get an ever-expanding, more accurate picture of the object you're looking at.

For example, in Genesis 1:1 the fourth word in English is a plural word, *Elohim,* in Hebrew. The word is translated "God" in English. By this name God let Adam and Eve know Him in what theologians call His "plurality in Unity" and in His creative power and Fullness of Might. In other words, this word has to do with the unity of His divine personality and power. God uses this name for Himself more than 2,300 times in the Old Testament.[1]

In Genesis 14:18, the second name of God is revealed, a singular word, *El,* translated "God Most High." This expands on His great power but also encompasses His "great and mighty promises." His being "the Strong One and first and only Cause of things" is brought to the front, as the singular case "emphasizes the essence of the Godhead."[2]

This one word *El* is compounded with other words

(e.g., *El Shaddai*) to reveal more and more, so that by the end of the sixth book of the Old Testament, it shows such characteristics as Everlasting, Almighty, Exclusive, a Jealous God, a Consuming Fire, Pitying, Merciful, Faithful, Living, and Most High, to name a few.

Through other names, the Scriptures later reveal to humanity the more personal, intimate qualities of God. But remember, God is infinite, and we are finite. So although we can get an excellent working knowledge of who God really is as we look at His names and then see His actions prove the validity of each name, we can never fully comprehend our wonderful God.

WHAT GOD'S NAME IMPLIES

Just as words cannot completely capture all that is involved in what we know by experience about a kiss, so we definitely cannot fully comprehend, explain, nor define "God." We can, however, look into His character by examining the third commandment on God's Top Ten List. Exodus 20:7 clearly states, "You shall not misuse the name of the Lord your God, for the Lord will not hold anyone guiltless who misuses his name."

In Hebrew thinking, a name represented a person's character, his personality. So if you want to learn how to be serious in your relationship with God, you will need to learn how to use His name correctly, because His name reveals who God is.

Sometimes we give our children a name that has a nice "ring to it." It wasn't that way in biblical times. People weren't given names because of the "sound." (If you heard some of those names—"Gomer," "Ichabod"—you would recognize right away this was the case.) Names were given to people for a reason. They had meaning, and a name often shaped the direction of that person's life.

Often, when a person sought a change of life or a change of behavior, or when God wanted to let him know he was being changed to a new level of service, it was accompanied by a change of name. Abram (high father) became Abraham (father of a multitude). Sarai became Sarah. Saul, the Jewish name, was changed to the Latin name Paul, since he was the Apostle to the Gentiles.

Let me suggest four aspects of God that will only be understood by knowing His names.

His Nature

God's nature is revealed in His name. Exodus 3:13–14 gives us a glimpse into this truth.

> Moses said to God, "Suppose I go to the Israelites and say to them, 'The God of your fathers has sent me to you,' and they ask me, 'What is his name?' Then what shall I tell them?" God said to Moses, "I AM WHO I AM. This is what you are to say to the Israelites: 'I am has sent me to you.'"

The name God gave to Israel to use to refer to Him was similar to their verb "to be." In Hebrew, I *am* was "Yahweh." We translate it "Lord" (all capitals) in our Bibles. The name implies existence—sheer, uncontrolled, unlimited self-existence. This is a reference to His infiniteness, His incredible power.

His Nearness

God's nearness is revealed in His name. One who seemed to know His nearness better than most was King David. He wrote a song on this very subject. Psalm 9:9–10 says, "The Lord is a refuge for the oppressed, a stronghold in times of trouble. Those who know your name will trust in you, for you, Lord, have never forsaken those who seek you." He also said in Psalm 139:7–10,

> Where can I go from your Spirit? Where can I flee from your presence? If I go up to the heavens, you are there; if I make my bed in the depths, you are there. If I rise on the wings of the dawn, if I settle on the far side of the sea, even there your hand will guide me, your right hand will hold me fast.

C. S. Lewis once said that we may ignore, but we can nowhere evade, the presence of God. The world is crowded with Him. To reveal to them His name of Lord meant that His presence was near.

His Reputation

God's reputation is revealed in His name. Why is it that David can say, "Those who know your name will trust in you"? Because they will know His reputation: "You . . . have never forsaken those who seek you." During a very difficult time in his life, King David penned Psalm 22, saying, "I will declare your name to my brothers; in the congregation I will praise you" (v. 22). What is meant by "declare your name"? This is explained by the second line of the verse: "I will praise you." What does it mean to praise someone? This means to brag, honor; to acknowledge and affirm. What is David saying? "When I get around my brothers, I'm going to tell them how great You are. I am going to behave in such a way as to honor Your good name and to increase Your reputation among this group of people."

His Relationship

God's name is so much more than a word. It implies His nature, His nearness, His reputation. But there's another thing it implies—something far greater. God's relationship is revealed in His name—His relationship with *us!* That God has given us His name is an awesome thing. In ancient times, it was believed that to know the name of a spiritual entity was to be able to control it in some way (through incantations, prayers, and spells). God made very clear that He could not be controlled. In fact His name implies it: "the self-existing one." As Paul the apostle said in a speech many years later:

> The God who made the world and everything in it is the Lord of heaven and earth and does not live in temples built by hands. And he is not served by human hands, as if he needed anything, because he himself gives all men life and breath and everything else. . . . For in him we live and move and have our being. (Acts 17:24–25, 28)

No, God was not to be manipulated by His name. This notwithstanding, to give the Israelites His personal name was clearly understood by them as in some way giving them His very self—His nature, His nearness, His reputation, and His honor. It was to open up to them a new level of relationship with Himself. "You can call me by My name."

Why should we take God's name seriously? Because His name reflects His nature and character; because His power and presence are very real; because of His reputation in our community; because to know His name is a privilege—it means that He desires to have a relationship with us.

If that's what "God's name" implies, then what's the point of the third commandment: "You shall not misuse the name of the Lord your God"? The point of this third principle is this: It's not just about *saying* God's *name;* it's about *showing reverence* for God's *nature.* To take God's name lightly is (1) to scorn His nature and character; (2) to underestimate His power and show contempt for His presence; (3) to misrepresent His reputation to the human family; and (4) to treat the awesome privilege of His relationship lightly. Such an offense is so serious that the principle is accompanied by a warning: "[Yahweh] will not hold anyone guiltless who misuses His name."

WAYS GOD'S NAME CAN BE MISUSED

Swearing

We misuse God's name when we use His name to swear at others. When we think about this commandment we most often think about profanity, swearing, or cursing. The dictionary defines swearing as "profanity; to show irreverence."[3] I think we all would agree that our society is full of profanity. I mean, it's obvious. Books, records, magazines, videos, TV. Today's comedians are garbage mouths. Virtually none say anything today without taking the Lord's name in vain. And people think it's funny. Swearing has become part of the nineties' lifestyle.

It amazes me that people who never pray, go to church, or read the Bible, and don't enjoy God, can't say a sentence without using His name. Many people do this because of their insecurity (seen most often in young people). Sadly, some people use God's name in vain so much that they don't even realize they are saying it. Using God's name improperly has become to them like "uh" or "well" is to others—a throwaway word with no significance. How sad to use something so special in such a careless and corrupted fashion.

Ever wonder why we don't say, "Oh, Hitler!" or "Oh, Satan!" I am convinced it is because the Enemy of our souls has purposely put it in man's heart to denigrate the holy name of God—to make it seem worthless and commonplace instead of something to be held in high honor.

Profanity has been defined as "weak people using strong words." It doesn't take a high IQ to swear. Parrots can be taught to curse. But a media-macho image is given to the person who swears. Tough cops in the movies curse. Aggressive athletes talk trash and blaspheme. The person who wants to get across his point of view in a strong manner does so by cursing. Why? I think people tend to swear out of a lack of emotional control. A person usually swears when he is uptight, frustrated, or angry. He gets cut off in traffic. He stubs his toe. He jams his thumb. It's really a demonstration of lack of control.

About now you might be thinking, *But Glen, I don't swear. How could I be misusing God's name?* Great question—inquiring minds want to know! Let me provide four additional ways you can misuse God's name for you to think through and apply to your life and language.

Excuses

We misuse God's name when we use God's name to make excuses. We attribute to God things He never wanted, or worse yet, things we really wanted. "I feel that God has called me to skip church today." "I don't feel that God wants me to help out." This can also show up in the form of blaming. We blame God all the time just to justify our desires. After all, He is the one who will excuse us for what we have done: "I know it's wrong, but God will forgive me." That is misusing God's name.

Intimidation

We misuse God's name when we use His name to intimidate others. Some people are pros at this. They use

God to back up their weak argument. God becomes their reinforcement. "God told me to give you this message." Whew . . . who is going to argue with God? "God has revealed to me what's wrong with you." (I have often wondered why God didn't tell me directly.) Some people act like they have a little handwritten note from God just for intimidation. Or how about the parent or friend who says, "If you don't do what I'm wanting, God won't be happy with you nor bless you." Many use God's name to try to get a person to do what they want.

When we use someone else's name for our personal benefit, it's called forgery. I wonder how many spiritual forgers we have who use God's name for their benefits! They take the Lord's name in vain by assuming His co-operation in their challenges. "If I don't get a million dollars by next week, I'm going to die." "I'm not leaving this chair until I get $100,000, so get on the phones." People all around us are turned off with church because they have been intimidated by God's name.

Showing Off

We misuse God's name when we use God's name to show off. Some people are spiritual show-offs. They want you to count how many times they say "Praise the Lord." Some people use spiritual-sounding language without even thinking about the words they say; their language patterns are an endless stream of religious clichés. Praise the Lord. Hallelujah. Bless His name. Glory to Jesus. Their minds may be in neutral, but they continually express their religiosity. Hey—it's OK to praise God, but are you using His name to impress? Some people advertise their Christianity for profit. "You can trust me . . . I'm a Christian."

Unthinking Responses

We misuse God's name when we use His name without thinking first. That's when we use it as a reaction to something. There are many ways we do this one. Many people use God's name as an exclamation—a "Wow!" or "Oh, no"—in response to something a friend says. "I just caught a five-pound trout." "Suzie's getting married." "I just split my pants." You know what that does? It reduces God to an exclamation point. You misuse His name when you say those kinds of things. The Bible says in 1 Samuel 2:30, "Those who honor me I will honor, but those who despise me will be disdained." Honoring God's name means you are taking Him seriously.

STEPS TO TAKE TO RESPECT GOD'S NAME

Obviously, God takes His name seriously, and so must we. The seriousness of this Top Ten commandment is demonstrated by God's indicating punishment is appropriate for misusing His name. What the punishment might be is left unsaid. That it would come is certain. This being understood, what are the appropriate steps we can take in our lives not only to take God more seriously, but also to fulfill this important commandment from God? Let's identify three ways.

Acknowledge the Privilege of Relationship

We can take God more seriously by acknowledging the privilege of His relationship. Many times we fail to fathom just how incredible it is to have a personal relationship with Almighty God. Perhaps we're familiar enough with God's name that this doesn't strike us as awesome or unusual.

Imagine that you were invited to a World Conference

of International Leaders at Camp David. You arrive and make your way past wave after wave of security cameras, security guards, and secret service agents. Finally you arrive in the room where they're meeting. A few members of the press corps privileged enough to be invited and an array of servants and security agents all speak to the world's power brokers in hushed, respectful tones, "Mr. President. Mr. Prime Minister. Mr. Chairman." A group of the leaders notices you and comes over, hands extended. You respond nervously, "Mr. President. Mr. Prime Minister. I don't understand . . ." "Enough of that," they say. "No formalities for you. We want you to call us Bill. Boris. John."

How would you respond? I don't know how I would respond, but I would understand that a new world of relationships had opened up. In giving me their names, they were extending to me the possibility of personal relationship—first-name basis. I would be blown away by the enormity of the offer, the unusualness, even inappropriateness. That scenario will never happen. But something greater *has*. Through Jesus Christ, the God of Creation, the Great "I AM," has extended His hand to you and me and has given us not only His name, but even more personally than that, has asked us to call Him Father.

The apostle John wrote, referring to Christ: "Yet to all who received him, to those who believed in his name, he gave the right to become children of God" (John 1:12). Have you ever come to the point where you've received that extended hand and accepted that relationship? Maybe for you to begin to take God seriously today is to accept that relationship. Perhaps you've received this relationship in the past, but have ceased to consider it an awesome privilege. You have taken it for granted. Ask God to help you have a stronger sense of awe about your relationship with Him. Try to express this in words as you talk with the Lord. The Scriptures, especially the Psalms, are a rich resource to find sentences and phrases that will help you express and develop a greater awe for your relationship with the God of the universe who wants a personal relationship with *you*.

Recognize His Power and Presence

Second, we can take God more seriously by recognizing His power and presence everywhere. We need to recognize that "the world is charged with the grandeur of God," as Gerald Manley Hopkins put it. This room you are reading this book in or the outside area you are enjoying right now is crowded with Him. As you drive home, your car or mini-van is crowded with Him. When you arrive at work tomorrow, the office is crowded. When you go to school this week, the classroom is crowded. As you face relational struggles at home (spouse, children), your home is crowded. As you face emotional, financial, moral dilemmas, if you have accepted Jesus Christ as your personal Savior, your life is crowded with His presence. The world is crowded with God. There is always a refuge for the oppressed, and always a stronghold in times of trouble. We can begin to take God seriously by recognizing, in general, His presence and power everywhere . . . and more specifically, His power and presence near me. Right here, right now. What is it that you're facing? What relational struggle? What emotional, financial, moral dilemma? He is there.

Increase His Reputation

Third, we can take God more seriously by increasing His reputation in our communities. God's name implies

His reputation. Your actions serve to either increase or decrease His reputation. Let me illustrate.

I can remember a woman in my church who was a "seeker." She had a genuine desire to know about God, had just started asking questions about the Bible, and was coming to our services regularly. A man at her work called himself a Christian. Everyone knew this. But everyone also knew that this man lacked integrity. In his speech and actions, he treated others with contempt. He cheated people; he cheated on his income taxes; he broke laws. This guy probably had no idea that his actions were having an effect on this woman and her understanding of God.

WAYS TO INCREASE GOD'S REPUTATION

How can you increase God's reputation among those who surround you? Four questions can be your guide.

Is there anything I'm doing to hurt His reputation? Any behavior that lacks integrity or moral uprightness? If God shows you something, confess it as sin and take the necessary steps to correct it. This may mean you will need to ask someone's forgiveness for your actions and the way you have misrepresented the Lord.

Is there anything I've done that I could rectify? Is there a person I've spoken harshly to and to whom I should apologize? A shady deal I should clean up? As with the previous point, do whatever it takes to rectify the wrongs.

Does this decision help or hurt God's reputation with those around me? Will other's think less of God or even blaspheme Him because of the choice I'm making?

Am I speaking highly of God when given the opportunity? Be careful to avoid preaching. However, perhaps you've noticed times you could have said something to honor Him, but haven't. Say something to reflect His goodness, kindness, and greatness. Ask the Lord to make you aware of future opportunities and to give you the right words to say. I like to ask at the beginning of my day for the Lord to show me where I can bring honor and glory to His name.

CONCLUSION

The tongue is a powerful tool entrusted to us by God. The Bible describes it as a flaming fire that can destroy and the rudder of a ship that can guide (James 3:4–6). How will you use your words to honor God's holy name and encourage others this week? I'm reminded of the story told about the surrender of the Confederacy at Appomattox Courthouse as the Civil War concluded. General Grant was an unusual man. Knowing the war was over and the victory was his, he showed great—and unusual—kindness and respect toward the chief general of the Confederates. He allowed General Robert E. Lee to ride freely in and out of the area. He also allowed the Confederate men to keep their possessions and horses. Grant gave them food because they were hungry and let them all go home undisturbed.

Lee was permanently touched by Grant's kindness. After the war, Lee took a job at Washington University in Virginia. On one occasion one of his fellow instructors, also a Southerner, began to speak poorly of Grant to Lee (assuming he'd receive a sympathetic audience). Lee turned, looked the man straight in the eye, and said, "Sir, if you ever again presume to speak disrespectfully of General Grant in my presence, either you or I will sever his connection with this university." Because General Lee had received such kindness from Grant, he treasured and protected the good name of the one who had showed him such kindness. So should we!

TOP TEN WAYS
TO TAKE GOD SERIOUSLY THIS WEEK

1. *Thank Him right now for the privilege of a relationship with Him.*
2. *Think of one thing you can do this week to enhance God's reputation in your surroundings . . . and do it!*
3. *Refuse ever to speak of or treat God lightly, even in jest.*
4. *Attempt to remain conscious of God's nearness throughout the day tomorrow.*
5. *Consider how God's power might help you face a current obstacle or dilemma.*
6. *Speak highly and freely of some of the great things God has done for you.*
7. *Take a walk in a park and consider the greatness of the One who made what you see.*
8. *Meditate on Scripture passages that speak of God's presence and power (Psalms 8, 23, 139; Romans 8:28–39).*
9. *Behave with complete integrity in your work, school, home, and community.*
10. *Close your eyes and think about God's character as you sing songs to Him in church this week.*

Notes

1. Herbert Lockyer, *All the Divine Names and Titles in the Bible* (Grand Rapids: Zondervan, 1975), 5–6.
2. Ibid., p. 7.
3. *Webster's New Compact Dictionary* (Nashville: Nelson, 1979), s.v. swearing.

chapter five

A Rested and Reverent Heart

"Remember the Sabbath day by keeping it holy. Six days you shall labor and do all your work, but the seventh day is a Sabbath to the Lord your God. On it you shall not do any work. . . . For in six days the Lord made the heavens and the earth, the sea, and all that is in them, but he rested on the seventh day."

—Exodus 20:8–11

The fourth commandment is "the only command not repeated after the day of Pentecost in the New Testament."[1] It is the only commandment for which a different reason for keeping it is given in Exodus and Deuteronomy (God's rest after creation, Exodus 20:11; God's deliverance of Israel from Egypt, Deuteronomy 5:6–21).

This commandment is both *for God* and *for man*. It is *for God* because He rested on the seventh day and set that day apart as holy. When we refrain from our daily work we are free to spend time on the Sabbath learning more about God and worshiping Him. By keeping the Sabbath we also proclaim that we believe He is strong enough to supply our needs even if we take a "day off" from our work.

It is *for man,* because it gives him a time for rest and recuperation from his everyday work. Jesus said, "The Sabbath was made for man, not man for the Sabbath. So the Son of Man is Lord even of the Sabbath" (Mark 2:27–28). Jesus also taught that it is righteous to do good on the Sabbath, even if that conflicts with a rigid observance of the Sabbath. "If any of you has a sheep and it falls into a pit on the Sabbath, will you not take hold of it and lift it out? How much more valuable is a man than a sheep! Therefore it is lawful to do good on the Sabbath" (Matthew 12:11–12).

BURNOUT

A man went to the doctor complaining of fatigue. He said he just felt tired all the time. The doctor asked him to try to identify the things in his daily routine that might be contributing to his condition. After some thought, the man wrote down five things on a piece of paper. The doctor took the piece of paper, studied it for a moment, said "Aha" and "Um-huh," and then wrote a prescription. He handed the prescription to the man, shook his hand, and wished him well. The man left the office with a great sense of relief. When he got into the car, he looked at the prescription the doctor had written. It simply said, "Don't do those five things."[2]

Have you noticed lately how tired people are? I see so many people through the week who just seem to be exhausted—physically, mentally, emotionally, and spiritually. The pace of their lives is killing them. They find it hard to keep their energy level up. They are simply "burned out."

Being burned out used to be tied to your age. The

older you were, the more tired you felt. The more years under your belt, the more vitamins in your cabinet. That doesn't seem to be true any longer. I used to think Geritol was for old people. Now the marketplace is full of products to make us peppy again. There are vitamins, hormone patches, special diets, high-powered drinks—all designed to perk up worn-out people.

A number of professions have high levels of burnout. Clergy are becoming the most vulnerable to burnout. Experience shows there are lots of worn-out preachers around. In fact, I wrote a book on this very subject called *Beyond the Rat Race.*[3] A recent article listed the top five reasons for clergy burnout:

1. Professional isolation and loneliness
2. Over-extension because of the insatiable needs of dependent people
3. An overload of demands—and an inability to balance congregational needs with personal and family needs
4. Having too many critics
5. Pressure to reach unrealistic goals and play too many roles[4]

In many respects, "ministry" as defined today has become too broad and unmanageable for just one person. Preachers burn out because people expect them to be proficient in too many areas. In a recent book I co-authored with Glenn Wagner, *Your Pastor's Heart,*[5] we made a chart of various responsibilities a senior pastor may have, such as sermon preparation, prayer, counseling, meetings, and planning. We then asked the reader to write down for each one how much time should be spent weekly on that particular responsibility. We strongly suspect that most readers will come up with eighty to one hundred hours of work per week for their poor pastors. Is it any wonder they never can satisfy everyone and are subject to burnout?

It's not just preachers who are worn out; churches are too. I've spoken to hundreds of pastors who have served some tired congregations in their time. I would venture a guess that most pastors' number one ministry issue is the church's need for resuscitation. The first job is to stabilize the patient, the church, and keep it from dying. Then, if the congregation makes it through the crisis, the next job is to begin the healing process that hopefully leads to health and wholeness. One of the reasons church planting has become such an appealing alternative to leaders is that they are personally experiencing burnout from constantly resuscitating dying churches.

THE REALITY OF STRESS

The next time you go to the market or the drugstore, take a look at the myriad products available for the treatment and relief of stress. These health products show the stressful condition of our day: Pepcid AC, Tagamet, herbal teas, and more. A recent study on stress by Johns Hopkins University says:

> Stress might not typically be thought of as a mental illness, but consider these facts from the American Psychological Association: 43 percent of adults suffer adverse health effects from stress; 75 to 90 percent of all physician office visits are for stress-related complaints; and in terms of lost hours due to absenteeism, reduced productivity, and worker's compensation benefits, stress costs American industry more than $300 billion annually. Stress also wrecks our health and our relationships and robs us of our happiness.[6]

Don't get me wrong. Not all stress is bad. It can be stressful to prepare for the holidays, but most people would not give up all the joy holidays bring in order to avoid stress. A dull job can often be more of a problem physically and emotionally than one that has a moderate degree of stress. Actors knows that if they do not have a little tension (stress) in their performances, they will risk giving a poor performance. Tension keeps one alert and better able to perform well than being too relaxed.

If we review secular approaches to stress relief, we discover some interesting approaches: mind control, relaxing exercises. But these don't necessarily help, although they may provide a temporary change of pace. What's the answer? How can we discover the skills necessary to implement the command to rest given in the fourth command of God?

GAINING THE REST YOU NEED

God never intended *burnout* to become a normal word in your vocabulary. Thus He provided us with another piece of the Big Ten puzzle:

> "Remember the Sabbath day by keeping it holy. Six days you shall labor and do all your work, but the seventh day is a Sabbath to the Lord your God. On it you shall not do any work, neither you, nor your son or daughter, nor your manservant or maidservant, nor your animals, nor the alien within your gates. For in six days the Lord made the heavens and the earth, the sea, and all that is in them, but he rested on the seventh day. Therefore the Lord blessed the Sabbath day and made it holy." (Exodus 20:8–11)

God takes the idea of rest very, very seriously, just as He takes the other Top Ten absolutes. But He felt so strongly our need to see the importance of rest that He modeled it for us in the rest He took on the seventh day, the day He finished all His creation. He set the standard by which we are to live and rest when He rested on the seventh day. But most of us feel that we can break this commandment without any fear of consequences. In fact, I wonder how many people I have heard bragging about their own busyness, workload, and stress levels. "Yeah, but Glen, I can rest when I get to heaven." Then why in the world did God give us this commandment? Why does this commandment contain ninety-four words, many more than the other commandments? No, the devil does not take a day off. But whose example do you want to follow—the devil's or the Lord's? Didn't our Lord say in Mark 2:27, "The Sabbath was made for man, not man for the Sabbath." There is a good reason for the Sabbath—for taking a day off. The reason? In part, it is so that we don't burn out. So let's look at some key principles that will enable you to get some rest.

Remember the Sabbath

The word *Sabbath* comes from the Hebrew word *shabath* and means "to cease, desist, or rest." In the South we might say, "Take ya shoes off and set a spell." Our kids might say, "Time for recess." A tech might advise you, "Stand by." Nehemiah said, "Don't work or sell" (see Nehemiah 13:15–22). I don't care how you say it: Take a day off, sleep a little later, eat a little lighter, take things a little easier—and spend time in the Word and in corporate worship.

I can remember living on a large lot in Southern California as I was growing up. There were lots of trees, ample places to hide, and wonderful space to play with toys that my children simply could not enjoy with the limited space they had growing up. One of those toys was a bow and arrow. My father was an outdoor kind of guy and so spent a lot of time explaining the safety rules and regulations I would have to follow if I was to contin-ue using this "adult" toy. One of those rules involved the unstringing of the bow so that it would last and main-tain its resiliency. This didn't make a whole lot of sense to me. Unstringing the bow meant that every time I wanted to play I was going to have to use every ounce of strength I could muster to restring the bow. I remember going out to the garage to get my bow after one extend-ed period of neglect and finding to my delight that I had not taken the string off. But then I saw that the bow had splintered right where I would have held it. I tried to tape it. That didn't work. I tried to splint it. No good! All I could do was lament about failing to relieve the pres-sure of the string and causing the bow to break.

Mark 6:31 says, "Then, because so many people were coming and going that they did not even have a chance to eat, he said to them, 'Come with me by yourselves to a quiet place and get some rest.'" Would you have gone? Or would you have come up with one of the myriad ex-cuses available in today's culture? "I'm too busy." Or how about the typical housewife response: "Too many people depend upon me for me to be able to take any time off." "I'm trying to do too many things to take some leisure time." "That wasn't scheduled on my Day-Timer." The old cliché about the last straw being the one that breaks the camel's back still is an accurate picture of the condition today of many burning-out people.

Evaluate Your Priorities

Matthew 16:26 says, "What good will it be for a man if he gains the whole world, yet forfeits his soul?" How easi-ly we can let this truth be ignored if we have our hearts

set on something we want. We will sacrifice almost anything for things—relationships, health, emotions. But the
one who wants to please the Lord will heed the instructions of 1 Timothy 6:6–7, "But godliness with contentment is great gain. For we brought nothing into the
world, and we can take nothing out of it." Isn't that true!
As many funerals as I've done, I've never seen a U-Haul
behind a hearse! If you kill yourself from overwork, burnout, lack of rest, what good has it done you? Your loved
ones whom you leave behind would far prefer to have you
than the money you worked yourself to death for.

REASONS WE IGNORE SABBATHS

So, why do people ignore the Sabbath day when we
all seem to want more time to rest and relax?

Ignorance

Some people have only seen workaholism modeled.
They don't know how to be *quiet*. Try an experiment
next time you are with a group of friends or family. Have
the whole room get very quiet and just listen to the silence. With our fast-paced life in the nineties in America, it seems unnatural to hear silence. Even in elevators
we have music, not to mention in our offices and shopping facilities. We really seem to be uneasy with quiet.

But God knows that we need times of quiet in our lives.
We need to be still. In Isaiah 30:15, He advises us, "In repentance and rest is your salvation, in quietness and trust
is your strength." Salvation is from the Lord, not from our
efforts. Do you believe this? Then it's time to act on it.

Greed

The love of money can drive us to work so hard that
we physically suffer. Not only are we warned that the

love of money is the root of all evil, but 1 Timothy 6:10 gives a further caution, "Some people, eager for money, have wandered from the faith and pierced themselves with many griefs." It is tragic to see someone who is strong in the faith and being used by the Lord get caught up in the desire to get money for the sake of acquiring things or financial security. As a pastor I've seen greed destroy ministries, families, and relationships. Thus, the Lord said in essence, "Follow My example. Rest one day a week."

Limited Resources

The opposite of greed can be need, or limited resources. But sometimes, we look at our limitations as being so overwhelming and our desires so great, that we are willing to sacrifice our day of rest in order to make the extra income to fulfill some of our desires. But God says He will supply all of our needs. We should trust that He has more than enough resources to meet our genuine needs. The one who is insecure in his finances reminds me of the kids on a farm, hoarding corn on the cob at dinner, afraid there won't be enough, when there are twenty acres of it just outside the kitchen window!

We really need to have God's perspective on the situation as David asked for in Psalm 90:12 (TLB), "Teach us to number our days and recognize how few they are; help us to spend them as we should."

FOUR RESULTS OF
VIOLATING THE SABBATH

Physical Breakdown

I have been told that the average life expectancy of a doctor is fifty-eight years. God designed humans to have a day of rest. I remember studying in school that earlier in this century men worked six days and rested one. The Communist Russians so hated the God of the West that they decided to go against the tradition of a Sabbath's rest every seventh day. They experimented with various models—seven days of work, one off; eight days with one off; etc. But much to their chagrin, they found that humans work best with six days of work and one of rest. So they were forced to return to the God-given pattern.

Mental Breakdown

The overload of stress causes our minds to be negatively affected. I know how it affects me. Add to stress the negative effects of being tired, and I slow down, feel like I'm a turtle in my thinking, and become prone to mistakes. Often I find it hard to think, and I make poor decisions. This condition just magnifies itself when I compound my exhaustion by not resting for many days in a row. Mentally I become a basket case both in performance and in my ability to control my emotions. When I am tired I am most likely to blow my relationships with others. My tolerance is low, my emotions under less control. I find myself too often in such situations wanting to do what is right, but not finding the ability to do so.

Spiritual Bankruptcy

As you cut back on your time with the Lord, you lose your spiritual health. How often as a pastor I've heard the excuses from people as to why they cannot regularly attend church, or if they do, why they cannot rest on Sundays. High on the excuse list of why people don't attend church is the statement, "I don't have any other day to rest except Sunday. This is the only time with the family." But they frequently don't rest on Sunday or even spend time with the family. So they compromise their Sabbath day of rest, because the Lord is not visibly standing in front of them, making His case for them honoring the Sabbath.

What I've also observed is that we take time for those things we value. I pastor a church of more than 1,600, speak at as many as thirty conferences and meetings across our nation each year, write one or two books a year, and have responsibilities as a husband and as a father to three young adult children, just to name a portion of my responsibilities. But experience has shown me that, as busy as I am, I am never too busy to squeeze in one more thing if I really want to, especially where my family is concerned. They are very high on my priority list and can knock out other less important activities if I so choose. When it comes to the Sabbath rest, the same principles apply even though I am a pastor. I have to decide that He is my top priority and I am going to protect my time with Him and His people.

Destroyed Mates and Kids

Too often people are not families; they are just relations that live under the same roof, each doing their own thing. Truly, the family that plays together stays together. It is important that quality recreation time be spent with family members. Remember, as parents you are modeling for your children how to be parents. If you do not model rest, they will end up as driven as you are. Keep a proper balance between work and rest.

When our lives get out of balance, and we overemphasize work to the detriment of other important things, then we can see the truth in the words of the wisest man on earth, Solomon, who put it this way in Ecclesiastes 2:22–23: "What does a man get for all the toil and anxious striving with which he labors under the sun? All his days his work is pain and grief; even at night his mind does not rest. This too is meaningless."

I may be able once in a great while to get away with not resting, but when this becomes a way of life, I am going to suffer. It really is true: Either we come apart to rest or surely we will come apart!

SOLUTIONS

I am, by calling and design, a problem solver. If my family has a problem, I will do everything in my power to solve it. Problem at church? Call Glen. Fortunately, there is an answer to this problem of rest, burnout, and spiritual stagnation. Let's look at the solutions.

1. Make Sure You Are Connected to the Power Source.

Too often people who are part of Christian churches, who have grown up in Christian families, are really not connected God's way to Him. God has a specific way we are to access Him, and that is only through Jesus Christ.

Pascal, the great French philosopher, knew this when he said that there was a God-shaped vacuum in the heart of every person that can only be filled by a personal relationship with Jesus. That is why Jesus says in John 14:6, "I am the way and the truth and the life. No one comes to the Father except through me." Many people know about Jesus, love Him, and ask regularly for Him to be with them and help them. But they have never, *in faith*, asked Him to come into their lives, to take control of their lives, and to make them what He wants them to be. This means trusting Him fully and therefore totally surrendering one's life to His control. God is a Spirit, and we need to cultivate an active spiritual life, communing with Him in prayer and learning about Him through study of the Bible (both at home and at church), worship at church, and prayer.

So make sure you have His life in you. How do you do that? Through a simple, heartfelt prayer, similar to the following:

> *Lord Jesus, I really need You. I can't live my life successfully without You. I am a sinner. I believe You died for my sins so I could be right with God and have His life—Your life—in me. So I am asking You to come into my life, forgive my sins, and make me the kind of person You want me to be. I surrender to You every area of my life. Thank You for hearing my prayer and for doing what I have asked.*

If you are not sure He is in your life, then you can pray this prayer or one of your own expressing these thoughts to Him. You can know that from this moment on you have Him in your life and that He will never leave you or forsake you (see Hebrews 13:5). When you have taken this step, then you will be connected properly to God as your Power Source.

2. Supercharge Your Soul.

My sons love to race remote-control cars. Scott is particularly good at building them and fine-tuning them. One of the major parts of a good racing car is a well-charged battery. If the battery is low, the car will not function efficiently. But sometimes the batteries need extended charges to bring the car up to being fully functional and highly effective. How does Scott know when the battery is low? The car will not run as fast. If he is not sure, he looks at the gauges.

This is my challenge to you: Check *your* three gauges. You may require an extended charge. Physically, are you fit and healthy? Spiritually, are you walking with God? Emotionally, are your emotions depleted or charged up? Jesus lived a life of balance—a lot of work followed by a time of going apart to rest. For although He was very God, He also was human, and humans need rest.

Paul says to forget the pattern of the world. We are prone to get caught up in the cultural mind-set and thus get squeezed into the mold of the world. But that mold is not appropriate for believers; we should not be comfortable in it. Instead he implores us in Romans 12:2, "Do not conform any longer to the pattern of this world, but be transformed by the renewing of your mind. Then you will be able to test and approve what God's will is—his good, pleasing and perfect will."

This is a fascinating passage. We are to renew our minds. How? When? Let me suggest that one key time is during your Sabbath rest. This is a time you can set aside to focus even more on the Lord. When we are not wrapped up in the world, in all the things that so easily entangle us, we can hear the still, small voice of the Spirit more clearly. It is He who will renew our minds through the Word.

But there are other important steps to being able to enjoy this wonderful refreshing from God:

3. Trust Jesus to Give You His Rest.

In Matthew 11:28–29, Jesus invites us, "Come to me, all you who are weary and burdened, and I will give you rest. Take my yoke upon you and learn from me, for I am gentle and humble in heart, and you will find rest for your souls." To take His yoke on us, we have to trust Him, to believe that He wants the best for us, and then do what He shows us to do. The wisest thing you can do when you find yourself weary and burdened is to take time to rest in God. Do not neglect the special day of rest God has provided for you. For rest from God is followed by peace from God.

4. Deal with Sin.

"Well, Glen, I've been a Christian for ten years and I still struggle with this recharging area. What am I doing wrong?" Let me return to Scott's batteries. One day Scott told me he needed new batteries. He went on to explain that despite the charger's being connected to the battery for an entire evening, the battery would not power up. After careful examination, Scott discovered corroded battery terminals were preventing a good charging. Sin is a lot like corroded terminals. It interferes with our connection to God and His power flowing in and through us. Is sin corroding your connection with God?

BENEFITS OF REST

Renewed Strength

Three benefits come from these times of rest. First, rest renews our strength. We need to have our "tanks" repaired and refilled. No vehicle and no human is designed to run without times of shutdown for rest, for a checkup, and for repair. Thus, rest helps us repair our physical and spiritual tanks wherever they may have gotten attacked or worn out, and then have them filled as we "wait on the Lord" during our Sabbath rest. This combination invigorates us and helps us face the new week prepared with His strength and directions. Isaiah calls this a time of waiting on the Lord (see Isaiah 40:31 KJV). The Lord promises that those who wait on Him "will renew their strength. They will soar on wings like eagles; they will run and not grow weary, they will walk and not be faint" (40:31 NIV).

Refinement of Character

Second, a time of rest can and will refine our character. It lets God tell us where our actions are not fully matching up to His standards, or where we have missed the mark. This time is crucial for our growth in character. In fact, Paul put it this way in Romans 5:3–4: "Not only so, but we also rejoice in our sufferings, because we know that suffering produces perseverance; perseverance, character; and character, hope." So even if the time of rest comes during a time of trouble, we can know that God has us going through a wonderful process. It is His will that trouble produces perseverance, which in turn produces valuable character in us. In times of trouble, it is very important to take a Sabbath rest, for it often is during such rest that God gives us the solutions to our problems. Often that includes changes in our character.

Renewed Purpose

Third, rest can refocus our purpose. During rest we can hear from God much better than when we are living at the fast pace of most of our lives. That is one key reason God gave us His day of rest. This is a time of recommitting ourselves to Him and His ways for our lives, of hearing His course adjustment for us.

David expresses in Psalm 42:11 what so many of us even as believers are experiencing in our fast-paced society. "Why are you downcast, O my soul? Why so disturbed within me? Put your hope in God, for I will yet praise him, my Savior and my God." We can only get downcast when we cast our eyes down. Keep them on the Lord. Focus on Him; take your day of rest so you can mount up with wings as an eagle and run and not be weary.

God wants the very best for us. He shows us how to get it, although we don't always follow what He shows. But when we do, we reap the benefits. And friends, believe me, the Sabbath rest is part of this benefits package God has for us. To ignore it is to suffer the natural consequences many of us are suffering—exhaustion, burnout, confusion, discouragement. But this is not God's game plan. That is why Jesus says in John 10:10: "I have come that they may have life, and have it to the full." Certainly if you are exhausted much of the time, your life cannot experience the richness, the fullness Jesus has for you, no matter how great the life is He offers. We have to have regular times of rest.

Notes

1. Charles Caldwell Ryrie, ed., *Ryrie Study Bible*, exp. ed. (Chicago: Moody, 1994), Exodus 20:8–11, n. See Colossians 2:16–17.
2. Kevin Conrad, "Surviving the Brave New World," *Sermon Notes* 4, no. 3 (May/June 1997 [issue 22]): 23.
3. Glen S. Martin, *Beyond the Rat Race* (Nashville: Broadman & Holman, 1995).
4. *1991 Survey of Pastors* (Pasadena, Calif.: Fuller Institute of Church Growth).
5. E. Glenn Wagner and Glen S. Martin, *Your Pastor's Heart* (Chicago: Moody, 1998).
6. Michael Clark, "Hopkins Q & A: Stress, Part One—Understanding the Problem," *Inteli Health* (7 November 1997), 1.

part two

loving your
NEIGHBOR

Then some of the Pharisees and teachers of the law came to Jesus from Jerusalem and asked, "Why do your disciples break the tradition of the elders? They don't wash their hands before they eat!"

Jesus replied, "And why do you break the command of God for the sake of your tradition? For God said, 'Honor your father and mother' and 'Anyone who curses his father or mother must be put to death.' But you say that if a man says to his father or mother, 'Whatever help you might otherwise have received from me is a gift devoted to God,' he is not to 'honor his father' with it. Thus you nullify the word of God for the sake of your tradition."

—Matthew 15:1–6

chapter six

Honoring Your Mom and Dad

"Honor your father and your mother, so that you may live long in the land the Lord your God is giving you."
—Exodus 20:12

The true story told by a woman demonstrates the frenetic pace of parenting. "When my child was six months old, I reentered the workforce. I was anxious about how I would juggle the morning chores—feeding and dressing the baby and myself, packing a lunch and the baby's bag, dropping her off at day care, and still getting myself to work on time. One frantic morning, I strapped the baby in the car seat and pulled out of the driveway ten minutes ahead of schedule. 'Mommy is so efficient,' I happily told my little girl. My smugness disappeared a few blocks later when I looked down and realized I was still in my bathrobe."

Mothers do a lot! They wear so many different hats: valet, taxi service, maid, financial planner, playmate, counselor, resident chef, and sometimes member of the marketplace. Often they do all of this and more with a minimum of recognition and appreciation. So do dads.

They take on the responsibility of providing security, the societal pressures of being the breadwinner. One little boy summed up the importance of his dad when in the midst of a lightning storm he called out, "Daddy, come. I'm scared!" The father said, "Son, God loves you and He'll take care of you." The little boy's reply was earnest and reflective. "I know God loves me. But right now I want somebody who has skin on."[1]

WHAT'S THE BIG DEAL?

As we come to the fifth commandment in God's Top Ten List, a noteworthy change of emphasis takes place. The first four principles focus on building a better relationship with God. We must put God first in our lives if we are to ever experience the kind of life God intended. We cannot replace God by images and idols representing a heart not in tune with God. We are to revere God's name and not take it lightly because it represents God's character. Then fourth, we are to honor and obey God by taking a sabbath rest, just as He did, so that we may be restored and refreshed in body and spirit and free to spend time in the Word and in divine worship. By keeping a sabbath, and not working that day, we are also saying that we trust God's provision to take care of our material needs.

The next six commandments focus on building better relationships with one another. It is not by coincidence that first of the final six is "honor your parents." Exodus 20:12 says, "Honor your father and your mother, so that you may live long in the land the Lord your God is giving you." To fully comprehend the meaning and practicality of this principle, I want to unpack four key points of understanding: the rule, the reason, the response, and the reward.

THE RULE

The rule is clear, *"Honor* your father and your mother." What does it mean to honor our parents over the course of our lives? Here are a few synonyms for *honor:*

- value highly
- care for
- show deep respect for
- obey

Now, it doesn't mean all these at once! Relationship changes through the years—and should! In our pre-adult years, God calls us to *obey* our parents. Ephesians 6:1 exhorts, "Children, obey your parents in the Lord, for this is right." Even the Lord Jesus demonstrated this obedience in His own life. In the passage describing our Lord's adolescent years we read, "Then he went down to Nazareth with them and was obedient to them" (Luke 2:51). Why was He always obedient? Because they were always right? No! Was His obedience based upon His parents' superior wisdom and moral integrity? No! Could it have possibly been that they knew more than He did? No! Our Lord's obedience was because God had given them to Him and He honored them. And therefore our Lord "grew in wisdom and stature, and in favor with God and men" (v. 52). So in preadulthood, *to honor* means *to obey with a proper attitude.*

In young adulthood, our relationship with parents begins to change. Unfortunately, too often as we believe we are maturing, we feel our parents have suffered brain damage.

Mark Twain said it best: "When I was a boy of four-teen, my father was so ignorant I could hardly stand to have the old man around. But when I got to twenty-one, I was astonished at how much he had learned in seven years."[2] At some directed time in life, children pass from a dependent relationship to an independent one, and so does the challenge of honoring. Honoring takes on the qualities of *respect* and *cooperation*.

It is essential, however, to understand that if you are to have a positive family relationship and to become a healthy adult yourself, you need to move past independence to interdependence. Proverbs 15:5 says, "A fool spurns his father's discipline, but whoever heeds correction shows prudence." The word *spurn* means to despise, cast off, or treat as worthless. As we pass from a relationship of dependence and obedience, our inclination is to spurn:

- To allow the pendulum to swing to the other extreme
- To despise, treat as worthless the role of our parents in our lives

This, Proverbs warns, is foolish, and, in fact, inhibits our progress toward emotional and spiritual adulthood. Instead of spurning, the wise and prudent teenager *heeds his parents' input*. This is the challenge of "honoring" in young adulthood.

When we arrive at adulthood, again there is a shift in the paradigm of honoring. Now to honor your parents is to *treasure* them. Proverbs 17:6 reflects this ideal, as generations grow in healthy relationships with one another. It declares, "Children's children are a crown to the aged, and parents are the pride of their children." Do you get a mental picture of the dynamic? Grandchildren are the reward of grandparents, just as each generation of parents is the pride of their children. Both statements speak of a mutual "treasuring," or honoring, that takes place.

As we enter the mature years of adulthood, however, the paradigm radically changes to one where we need to begin to *appreciate* our parents. Often only as we become parents ourselves do we recognize and appreciate all that was done for us. Only then do we realize that there are phases of learning. We will grow as we recognize the similarity between our youthfulness and our children's youthfulness. My mother always said to me, "Glen, I hope you have a child just like you were so you can understand what I had to go through." Well, Mom, I had three of them.

Ironically, the older our parents get, the less our society appreciates them. They can't work anymore, and so they begin to question their personal worth and influence. At the same time we are going through the busiest time of our lives. It is easy to forget parents, not from independence, but busyness. To honor our parents through this phase means to appreciate them, to value them and communicate with them. Sometimes, it also means caring for them, helping them look down the road and provide for future needs.

As I went through the final editing of this book, my wife, Nancy, was devoting an enormous amount of time caring for her mother, Mary, who was suffering from terminal lung cancer. Nancy's mom had always been so independent, so strong, a model of strength and perseverance. After five successive treatments of chemotherapy, it became apparent the fight was nearly completed. Nancy's role immediately changed. Now Nancy was the caregiver, along with her sister, Nora, rather than a care-receiver. Nancy became the encourager, the strength, the stabilty. The roles had reversed very quickly.

"Honor your parents!" What does this mean? Different things at different times. Here's the general rule I offer to fully incorporate this part of God's Top Ten into your life, for this is always true:

> Honoring your parents is an attitude accompanied by actions that says to your parents: "You are worthy. You have value. You are the person God sovereignly placed in my life. You may have failed me, hurt me, and disappointed me at times, but I am taking off my judicial robe and releasing you from the courtroom of my mind. I choose to look at you with compassion and respect—as people with needs, concerns, and scars of your own."[3]

THE REASON

Why is this commandment so important? *Can't I just skip this one?* No, you can't. And here's why. First, *parents are our most influential relationship.* Studies in childhood development are showing now that, for the most part, our personalities, behavioral patterns, and relational styles are set by age six. Most people do not like thinking that brief phase of their lives had such a powerful influence on them. "I am not set in *stone.* I'm simply really hard *clay.* Through some hard work, things can be reversed." That's not necessarily true. Through the grace of God we may all change, but it is still true that much of what we are like was established early in our lives. It also bothers some people that parents can have such a strong influence on their kids. But it is still true that parents are the most influential relationship in our lives, whether through negative elements, including dysfunction and insecurities, or through the positive ones: our strengths, abilities, and gifts. We are who we are largely because of our parents.

The second reason for not skipping this commandment is that *parents reflect all authority.* Why is this relationship so influential in my life? I've discovered that the way I respond to my parents shapes the way I respond to others and, in particular, to authority.

Consider a counselor's interaction with a man named Ralph.

Ralph was 28 when he came to see me for counseling. He had been fired from almost every job that he ever had. "Why does this happen?" I asked him. "Well, those guys always order me around like I'm a nobody. I can't stand to be talked to like that. So, I decide, 'I'll show them,' and then I do." "But it always costs you your job. Is it worth it?" I asked. "Every time," he said definitively. "I'll never bow down to them that way. Nobody will ever do that to me again." "Do what?" I asked. Ralph began to shake with anger. As we talked further, he described years and years of angry abuse at the hand of his authoritarian father. Hating all authority figures with a passion, he had not been able to learn to submit to them or act authoritatively in his own life. He was still an angry little boy in a power struggle with his father.[4]

Our parents represent the first and most important line of God-given authority. If we never learn to respond appropriately to that authority (even when it is abused), we will not likely respond well to other authority figures in our lives, even to God's authority. And to that extent, we will not become the spiritually and emotionally whole people God created us to be.

But let's look even deeper at this principle. We are told that we are to obey our parents *so it can go well with our lives and that we will live long lives.* You may think, *Why should my life be longer if I obey my parents?*

The answer lies in the respectful mind-set. The young person who does not respect authority, who disobeys his parents, usually also has a low regard for civil authority, such as the police or even speed limits and stop signs. He often is the one who runs red lights and zooms past you on the freeways, doing many miles over the limit. Such a person likes taking unnecessary risks, pushing the limits, and in general putting himself in harm's way more frequently than the one who respects authority because he has learned to do so in his family.

But notice the cultural setting here. Obedience to parents is good "so that you may live long *in the land the Lord your God is giving you.*" Remember, the Ten Commandments were originally given to Israel (although all but the Sabbath are repeated in the New Testament as God's expectations for us today). Israel had been delivered from Egypt. God was now going to give them a land of their own. Before He did, He gathered them around this mountain and said, in effect, to them: "Do you want to make this thing last? Do you want to pass it on to your kids and their kids? Then it's essential that this new society gets this pivotal principle right: Honor your parents. Treat them with respect and value." Although we can see the practical application of this, as a promise this is probably not about long life for each individual, but about longevity as a nation in the land they would enter.

The third reason for this commandment never to be skipped is that *parenthood is honorable.* Perhaps the basic truth of this has escaped us in this advanced age. No longer is parenthood valued as a significant contribution to society. We're valued instead for how much money we make, how much stuff we own, how good we look. In this setting, it shouldn't surprise us that "honoring our parents" seems like an archaic value. Yet there are few things as significant as the role of parents.

There is a degree to which we should all view the relational impacts we make in our lives as a priority over the vocational impacts. After all, relationship is what God is all about, and what He wants us to value. Our vocation is a calling, gives us fulfillment, and provides a way to meet daily needs. But too often we pour our life, our time, and our energy into our vocation and neglect our relationships.

In our modern society, where we no longer have the extended family unit, many adults have older parents who are neglected and have to spend their twilight years alone and feeling useless. In the extended family as seen in Old Testament times, older parents were there for their children, which helped both generations. The mother was available to ease the load of her daughter or daughter-in-law. She was able to pass on her years of wisdom and her expertise in handling children, and she could even be a baby-sitter to lighten the pressures on her children and their spouses, since she would live with or very near them. Parenting, as God designed it, is very honorable.

THE RESPONSE

What should be our response to this commandment? This is tough to answer. It may be true that change is never easy, but growth in our personal lives and our spiritual lives demands we change. What are some ways we can put this important principle into action in our lives?

Become Honorable Parents

Rodney Dangerfield's words can also be said of parenting: "I don't get no respect." Perhaps the best way to "end the cycle" is to reverse it in your own life. Are you behaving in an honorable way? Do you:

- Behave with integrity at home and at work? Do your kids see that?
- Model respect for your parents to your kids? Speak well of your parents and mention their good points? Help your kids understand the reasons behind any negative behavior toward them by their grandparents?
- Have a healthy attitude toward other authority figures? Obey civil laws, such as in driving? Pay your taxes on time?
- Treat authority figures and those under you with respect? Ask God to give them and you self-control when needed.

Express Your Appreciation to Your Parents

Sounds simple, doesn't it? Yet when was the last time you said thanks to your parents? When was the last time you told them you loved them? You may find yourself, like many good believers, struggling with saying one or both of these things to a parent because of your negative history with that parent. We'll look at that in a minute, but no matter what your history is, the present should be approached with the desire to honor your parents if for no other reason than it is the right thing to do and it will be in line with God's command.

But it is also emotionally healthy for you to express your appreciation to them. They sacrificed a lot to get you grown up. They could have abandoned you or thrown you out. And maybe they did. In that case, the next point is vitally important for you to have any hope of "honoring your parents."

Ideally we should have strong, healthy relationships with our parents. But in reality, our history with them can affect our ability to express sincere appreciation to them. I have found *The Blessing,* by Gary Smalley,[5] to be a wonderful tool in expressing approval to parents. It helps you find positive areas to comment on no matter how much they may have missed the mark in parenting. This brings us to the crucial need for forgiveness.

Practice Forgiveness

Some of you may have issues with your parents that make it hard to honor them. So you may need to learn to practice forgiveness. As I've counseled through the years, I've seen that feelings can be a big hang-up for many people. They think that in order to give forgiveness they need to feel it first. In reality, feelings are simply emotions, and emotions usually follow an act. So don't put your cart of feelings before your horse of forgiveness. Offer the forgiveness in obedience to the Lord. The feelings may or may not follow. If you know you still have unforgiveness, let me suggest several things to do. If you are willing to have God help you forgive, go directly to Step #2 below. If not, then go to Step #1.

Step #1

Admit to God your unwillingness or inability to forgive. Tell Him you simply cannot bring yourself to forgive your parents(s) because of (and then list out the offenses). Write them all out on a piece of paper. Next, write Matthew 6:14–15 across the list.

Now ask the Lord to help you to be willing to forgive them. As part of this step, think about all the terrible things you have done in your life that He has forgiven on the cross.

Next, meditate on His statement in Matthew 6:14–15 that if you do not forgive others, then you will not receive forgiveness. How does this truth apply to your current situation? Are you satisfied to keep a barrier between you and the Lord just to have revenge on your parents? Remember, the Enemy of your soul does not want you to forgive. He wants to keep you a prisoner. Don't let him win. The Lord will show you the truth and will help you get the victory over your feelings.

But know that feelings are not the important thing in God's eyes. Your obedience is. Your feelings have different levels of holds and expression in your life, with the strongest, deepest roots of unforgiveness being the source of emotional death in your life. To offer forgiveness is to cut those deepest roots, even though you may not be aware of the effects at first. Even after these have been cut, the lesser, more surface feelings of hurt may remain as a parent who is still living keeps heaping on you more and more abuse. But when you have offered God's forgiveness, such a parent cannot damage you at this deepest level if you don't let him or her.

Now, see if you have enough courage and freedom from the Lord to be able to go on to Step #2. Claim God's promise in Philippians 4:13, which says that you can do all things through Christ who strengthens you.

Step #2

Once you have come to the point that you are willing to forgive any and all wrongs done to you by your parents, the next step is *to actually give the forgiveness.*

First, you need to get things right with God. You can pray something along these lines:

Father, I ask You to forgive me for all the years of unforgiveness and the dishonoring of my mother/father. I am now ready to obey Your command to honor them. So I choose to forgive my mother/father for (name the offenses), not because they have earned the right to my forgiveness, but because I love You so much that I am doing this in obedience to You.

Next, you need to ask the Lord to show you how to honor your parents. Some ideas in the first step in practicing forgiveness may help. As part of this, ask Him to let you see your parents as He sees them and to help you to feel toward them as He does by giving you His love and compassion for them.

Then, as He does this, don't resist it because it is so unnatural to your previous way of thinking about them. Choose, as an act of your will, to say good things about them.

Ask the Lord to put a check on your thoughts and words. Part of the "forgiveness" package is to "take captive every thought to make it obedient to Christ" (2 Corinthians 10:5). This means that when a negative thought pops into your head about your parent(s), you recognize that this is not what you or God wants you to think about them, and you reject the thought the Accuser of the Brethren has tempted you with. By not taking ownership for the thought, you are resisting the development of any new strongholds of unforgiveness or even a critical spirit.

Step #3

Right prayer has amazing power for change. I have found that *praying positively for my parents* has not only affected them, but has been used of the Lord to help change my heart toward them in areas where my attitude has been wrong. I ask Him to bless them, to minister to them, to strengthen and encourage them, and to help them draw closer to Him. I ask that each day will be one in which they are able to see and receive His blessings. As part of this, I have asked the Lord to give me specific verses to claim for each one.

Praying appropriate Scripture for your parents can be powerful both for you and for them. It helps, also, to get your eyes off your parents, and onto the Lord who is in control in your situation.

Pursue Emotional Reconciliation with Your Parents

Maybe you're thinking, "You don't know my parents. You don't know what they did to me." You're right. I don't. But God does. And He is the One who wants you to forgive them. In fact, He makes His preference in this matter so strong that He says you are to forgive others because of all that God has forgiven you. He does not give you any room on this one. You may have experienced physical or emotional abuse, even molestation. But the Lord is clear. Forgive. He accepts no excuse for not forgiving. What's more, as we've noted, He says that if you do not forgive others, then you will not receive forgiveness (Matthew 6:14–15; Mark 11:25).

I am not talking out of theory here. I have seen firsthand the results when parents do things that cause their children deep pain. You may have been talented, but could never please your parents. Your straight "A's" were not praised, but your sister's "B's" and "C's" always were. When you were in your teens you may have had a disagreement with your parents so strong that it caused you to leave home. Your parents may not have liked the fact that church had become a major influence in your life, or they may not have approved of the person you were dating—even though that person later turned out to be your spouse of more than a quarter century. You may never have been able to fully break down the wall between yourself and your parents. But all of these injustices do not excuse you from holding onto the pain, for nursing the hurt, for living in unforgiveness. Why? The reason is twofold.

First, think for a minute. If you are still holding something against your parent(s), do you have freedom in your life, or is this unforgiveness holding you a prisoner? You may not recognize it, but if you are living with unforgiveness, you *are* a prisoner. It is inevitable.

But more important, to live in unforgiveness is to live in sin. As we have seen, God gives us no option. Even if we could not recognize a human need to forgive and reconcile, we still need to do so because God has said to. It is part of our obedience and submission to Him and a proof of our faith and trust in His ways being right and just and the best thing for us.

There is more we can do to pursue reconciliation beyond forgiving them. We can choose to honor them. We can think back over all the good things they have done for us, all that even in their flawed behavior they were able to instill in us. It may be that our sufferings have raised our own level of compassion and understanding and ability to counsel others with similar problems. Because this is true, we can do the second thing, which is to thank God that He makes everything work together for good.

As part of this step, we can recognize that to honor our parents will never mean to agree with all of their decisions, or to approve of or thank them for their negative behavior. But it does mean to respect them, to value them enough as human beings to pursue reconciliation.

How blessed is your situation if it is possible to work through this with your parents.

You may not have that possibility. You can, however, still act honorably by continuing to pursue emotional reconciliation with your parents, and after doing all the Lord shows you to do, leaving it in His hands. It is not for nothing that society has the idiom, "You can lead a horse to water, but you can't make him drink." You be certain you have led your parents to the waters of forgiveness. If they refuse to drink, that is between them and God. You will have done all you can and all God expects from you.

However, do be aware that the Enemy will try to make you critical of them if they have rejected you. Don't let him win. Instead, ask the Lord to show you your parents as He sees them, to give you a love for them that is His love for them. In this way you can have a pure heart before the Lord and may even develop a compassion and understanding of the hurts they received that spilled over to you.

Often in counseling I suggest that people think back to their parents' parents and even great-grandparents, to see if there was a lack of the modeling of right parenting in previous generations. For if your parents had no model, and only a flawed pattern to imitate, how difficult it would be for them to be other than they are apart from the Lord's intervention.

As we look at forgiveness and giving thanks, for some the wounding may be so deep, the offense so great, that the only good that has come from it is the ability the wounded person developed to see the face of the Lord throughout it. This has helped the person survive the experience. A book by Glenda Revell, *Glenda's Story*, may be helpful here.[6]

THE REWARD

But to be driven closer to the Lord, to see His goodness and faithfulness in the worst of times is something to value, yes, even to treasure. It reminds me of the spirit of Helen Keller who should, from a human perspective, have had zero to be thankful for as a blind and deaf woman. Yet God could and did turn even such a devastating handicap into a beautiful instrument that shaped her life to be used in a unique way in the lives of others as few have had the privilege of doing.

Or an even closer parallel is that of Corrie ten Boom who learned to forgive the Nazi prison guard who was, in part, responsible for her beloved sister's death.

Earlier we talked about the promise that goes with the command to honor our parents: "That you may live long in the land the Lord your God is giving you" (Exodus 20:12). That is a part of the reward of honoring our parents. We are promised the benefits of a long and fulfilling life. There is also a social longevity related to how we treat our parents. If we as a Christian community want to last long, and more broadly speaking, if we as a nation want to last long, this is a principle we would do well to learn.

TOP TEN WAYS
TO HONOR YOUR PARENTS THIS WEEK

1. *Treat your mom and dad to something special.*

2. *Encourage grandparents to tell your children stories of "the good old days."*

3. *Send a video of yourself or your family to distant parents and grandparents.*

4. *Forgive your parents for the mistakes they may have made.*

5. *Ask their advice on a tough issue you're facing . . . and listen!*

6. *Take your children to see them.*

7. *Discuss ways to care for them as they age.*

8. *Model respect for them to your children.*

9. *Call them and thank them for their sacrifices in raising you.*

10. *Tell them they are valuable to you and you are praying for them.*

Notes

1. Michael P. Green, *Illustrations for Biblical Preaching* (Grand Rapids: Baker, 1989), 147.
2. *The Great American Bathroom Book,* vol. 1 (Salt Lake City: Compact Classics, 1991), 178.
3. Dennis Rainey, as quoted in *Better Families* 19, no. 3 (March 1995).
4. Henry Cloud, *Changes That Heal* (Grand Rapids: Zondervan, 1990), 219.
5. Gary Smalley and John Trent, *The Blessing: Giving and Gaining Family Approval* (Nashville: Nelson, 1986).
6. Glenda Revell, *Glenda's Story* (Grand Rapids: Revell, 1994).

chapter seven

Dealing with Your Anger Problem

"You shall not murder."

—Exodus 20:13

While W. C. Fields lay on his deathbed, a friend stopped by to see him and was surprised to find him reading the Bible. As you probably know, W. C. Fields was a lot like the rascally, drunken characters he often portrayed. The friend asked, "Why in the world are you reading the Bible? Are you looking for answers?"

W. C. Fields said, "No, I'm looking for loopholes."[1]

One way or another, Mr. Fields found out there are no loopholes in the Bible. Its truth is far-reaching, long-lasting, and absolute. When God provides input and insight into our lives, it will do us well to listen and learn. But when we hear the words of our Lord, there are times when they cut us to the core and we find ourselves looking for loopholes. Probably one of the statements many people have trouble following is what Christ said regarding the sixth item on God's Top Ten List: "You shall not murder" (Exodus 20:13). Jesus said that even if we haven't actually intentionally murdered someone by violently taking a life, if we harbor hate toward that person there is a sense in which we have actually killed him. In God's eyes murder encompasses far more than physically taking someone's life. Jesus gave us insight into the broader scope of the term *murder* as He addressed this topic in Matthew 5.

Here is recorded one of the greatest sermons ever given. It came from Jesus as He sat on the side of a mountain. Jesus began with a discussion of happiness as He revealed who the people are who are going to be blessed—the poor in spirit, the gentle, the merciful, and those who hunger and thirst for righteousness. He next challenged His followers to shine (like light) and provide flavor or preservation (like salt) to a lost world.

Then, suddenly, Jesus shifted gears to address some of the elements in the Father's Top Ten List.

> "You have heard that it was said to the people long ago, 'Do not murder, and anyone who murders will be subject to judgment.' But I tell you that anyone who is angry with his brother will be subject to judgment. Again, anyone who says to his brother, 'Raca,' is answerable to the Sanhedrin. But anyone who says, 'You fool!' will be in danger of the fire of hell. Therefore, if you are offering your gift at the altar and there remember that your brother has something against you, leave your gift there in front of the altar. First go and be reconciled to your brother; then come and offer your gift." (Matthew 5:21–24)

Because His hearers were congratulating themselves for how well they believed they kept the commandments, our Lord shifted the emphasis from one perception of murder to another, from the concept of *literal* murder to an ongoing reality in our lives—anger, a subtle form of murder that kills the soul, the spirit. The word *Raca* was an Aramaic insult meant to demean a person and denigrate his character. It was said in such a way as to almost spit on the person you had addressed. The term had nothing to do with a person's IQ, abilities, or standards. He was simply worthless in the eyes of the critical person.

Our Lord takes us by the collar, stands us up, and looks us squarely in the eyes to say, "Listen, it is just as evil to hurt the dignity and worth of another person as it is to murder him." In the eyes of our Savior, to put down another person—someone God created and Jesus died for —is just as violent as taking that person's life. God has made everyone in His image and has a tremendous future in store for each one of us.

Why the intensity of Jesus' statements? Several reasons. Through the grid of God's love and acceptance, to denigrate a person is an insult in two ways to the Creator who formed him in His image. First, it is to reject God and His image as reflected in that person. Second, it is to reject God's handiwork and purposes through that individual.

Genesis 1:27 reads: "So God created man in his own image, in the image of God he created him; male and female he created them." God has a reason for every breath and heartbeat we have been given. God has a purpose for every life He created. In fact, there is not a person whom God does not love. So to degrade a person is to fail to see his or her worth in God's eyes.

The second piece of the puzzle I believe our Lord was addressing in His commentary on the sixth commandment is the fact that hatred toward someone may cause just as much damage to that person's life as physical abuse would. Alan Loy McGinnis tells a tremendous story about a support group in his book *The Friendship Factor*.

In one of our therapy groups we were discussing body image, and different people were telling how they saw themselves. A tall, slender young woman with beautiful long
hair said: "I see myself as fat and pimply." "You mean you
used to be fat with pimples?" someone asked. "No, that's
how I see myself now." If anything, the lady was skinny,
and she had fine, clear skin. . . . Here was a gorgeous
woman who did not know she was beautiful because no
one was telling her.[2]

Some have perpetuated the falsehood, "Sticks and
stones may break my bones, but words will never hurt
me." When I was young, I would say this, even sing it,
but I never really believed it. Neither did you! Maybe you
were the one who was told you were too fat, too tall, too
smart, too short, too clumsy, too Goody Two-shoes. You
may have been the person who was the last one picked
on the lunchtime teams, or you were never picked for the
team. You spent the majority of your lunch hours sitting
on the sidelines, alone and abandoned. Rejection is extremely painful, and you can have your self-worth murdered by demeaning, angry words hurled at you. James
3:9–10 says, "With the tongue we praise our Lord and Father, and with it we curse men, who have been made in
God's likeness. Out of the same mouth come praise and
cursing. My brothers, this should not be."

YOU LOSE!

Is anger really that big a deal? Yes!

- Family members are hurt by your words and actions.
- You feel large amounts of guilt and experience self-
  hate because you can't control your anger and are
  ashamed of the effect your anger has had on the
  lives of those you have hated.

- Unrest and turmoil are in your heart because of unresolved and/or uncontrolled anger.
- Walls are built between you and others.
- Fellowship with God is weakened.
- Long-term damage to your walk with the Lord can occur.
- Your health—emotional and physical—can be damaged.
- You can permanently damage others, yourself, and property.
- You can permanently damage your marriage and other relationships; this damage can even lead to divorce.

FOUR COMMON MYTHS ABOUT ANGER

In speaking for Promise Keepers, I have spent much time talking to men about the issue of anger. And I think I have heard every excuse and rationalization for anger, while the parties who are giving the excuses never get to the root of the problem. Here are four myths I have heard consistently.

Myth #1: "Venting my anger is always healthy."

If you look at a two-year-old's way of dealing with anger, you find tantrums are common. In fact, we speak of parents "surviving" the "terrible twos." Any parent realizes that either (1) a transition will take place as the child matures and the parents help the child learn to control such behavior, or (2) the child will grow up continually dealing with anger by venting or throwing a tantrum. Uncontrolled anger reveals immaturity or damaged emotions as well as an unwillingness to deal with the anger by finding a solution.

Myth #2: "Talking out anger gets rid of anger."

Not true! Expressing your anger is not necessarily going to remove your anger, just as pouring gasoline on a fire will not put it out. Sometimes you need to evaluate what kind of anger you are feeling and whether or not you desire to stay angry. Ask yourself why you are angry and what part of the problem is your responsibility and what part is the responsibility of the other person. Often we find we are angry for no valid reason. We blow up just because we get frustrated and don't know how else to respond. We will be looking later at how to deal with different types of anger.

Myth #3: "Aggressive behavior will eliminate anger."

That's just not true. It escalates your anger. I wonder how many times I have heard in church about a person who was angry and became verbally or even physically aggressive, and someone says, "Oh, that's just the way so-and-so is all the time." Just because repeated fits of anger are a habit for you doesn't make it right. Your aggression against others feeds your anger rather than starving it.

Myth #4: "Anger has no effect on my health."

Study after study has proven this not to be true. Dr. Dean Ornish has researched this very subject. In the book *Anger Kills,* he describes a trial study in which the subjects were

> forty-one heart patients with coronary artery blockages severe enough to cause their heart muscles to be starved

for blood. These patients were randomly assigned to routine cardiology care or to a comprehensive treatment program that included dietary fat restriction, exercise, yogic relaxation training, and group sessions designed to improve their ability to cope with stress. Compared with the nineteen subjects in the routine care group, the twenty-one in the special intervention group showed actual shrinkage of their coronary artery lesions and improved heart-muscle function—without drugs or surgery.[3]

In addition to the benefits of diet, meditation, and exercise, Ornish believes strongly that the patients' improved ability to handle stress, which he ascribes to the social support provided by the group sessions, "was a key ingredient in the treatment program's success."[4] In other words, anger and forms of hostility were a part of what was killing these people.

We are all at risk of giving in to these myths. Some will say, "Yes, anger kills," but soon follow with, "but it won't kill me." Living in denial doesn't heal. If I have a toothache, I can deny its reality all I want, but the dull ache will eventually consume me if I do not take action. Uncontrolled anger often leads to murder. Rage and revenge are dangerously close to crossing the line that will end in murder. So God warns us to take control of our emotions before they destroy us.

FOUR TYPES OF ANGER

You may have heard how captive elephants are trained not to try to escape. Baby elephants are chained to stakes driven deep into the ground. The baby elephants don't grasp the limitation placed on them and are unaware of how little strength they have, and so they attempt to get away. They pull and tug on the rope or chain, sometimes bruising or cutting themselves, until they recognize they are not going anywhere. So they quit trying. As the elephants grow up, they remain conditioned to the limitations placed on them by the chain, despite the fact that in their adult strength they could easily pull the stake out of the ground. But if they smell smoke with their very own nostrils and see flames with their very own eyes, they will move. You can count on it!

Maybe you, like some people, need to smell the smoke and see the flames of your own personal anger. Your friends have felt your anger, your family is fearful of your anger, and you remain conditioned not to try to break away from these tendencies because "I've always been like this." You need to smell the smoke and see the flames by examining four typical types of anger as seen in the Bible.

Radical Anger

The people who commonly exhibit radical anger are always on the verge of blowing up. The fuse is lit, just waiting for the right place and person to explode upon.

Radical anger happens more often than we care to admit. Cain, in the Old Testament, struggled with this. In Genesis 4:5, 8, we read:

> But on Cain and his offering he [God] did not look with favor. So Cain was very angry, and his face was downcast. . . . Now Cain said to his brother Abel, "Let's go out to the field." And while they were in the field, Cain attacked his brother Abel and killed him.

Cain did not deal with the real issues in his life; instead, his radical anger got the best of him.

We see a clear example of this today in what we label "road rage." Living in Southern California where there is an epidemic of this type of anger, I've seen many a driver express great anger at the actions of other drivers.

It is not unusual to read in the papers or see on the news that someone has been shot because he cut off another driver or did something else to enrage an assailant. In fact, truckers have been known to crush offending cars.

Repressed Anger

People who operate with repressed anger just hold the anger in, swallowing the pain. Swallowing a hurt means your stomach gets to keep score. This kind of anger will destroy a family, marriage, or relationship from the inside out.

I believe Job had to wrestle with this kind of anger. Early in the book of Job, his world fell apart. He lost his health, his family, and his wealth. How would you have reacted? "That's not fair, God! What did I do to deserve this? What about so-and-so? They aren't living the way you want—get *them!*" Not Job. With eloquence he said, "Naked I came from my mother's womb, and naked I will depart. The Lord gave and the Lord has taken away; may the name of the Lord be praised" (Job 1:21).

Well, along came some of Job's friends (if this is an accurate term for those folks). They told Job how sinful his life must have been for all these bad things to happen to him. He was confronted by Zophar concerning the direction of his heart. Suddenly, Job's anger began to show. He even redirected his own anger toward God.

> "Though I cry, 'I've been wronged!' I get no response; though I call for help, there is no justice. He has blocked my way so I cannot pass; he has shrouded my paths in darkness. He has stripped me of my honor and removed the crown from my head. He tears me down on every side till I am gone; he uproots my hope like a tree. His anger burns against me; he counts me among his enemies." (Job 19:7–11)

Repressed anger allows me to get angry with God, but even then I will suppress anger because "good people don't get angry with God." I am convinced Job's problem was a subtle form of works we don't recognize as sin. He felt he had *earned* God's favor, had done all the "right" things, and therefore should not have been under such an attack. What you see is a classic case of a man starting out with the right attitude ("If I receive good from God, should I not also accept the bad, too?") that turned into a bad attitude the longer he sat there, suffering, seeing no end to his misery and negative situation. Certainly no one else was reaching out to genuinely help him. Even his best friends were heaping unjust criticism and accusations on him. So the longer he sat there, the more he allowed his "fate" to be the focus of his attention, until finally he took his eyes off the Lord. Then he reached the low point of cursing the day he was born and wanting to argue with God.

I've found myself doing the same thing as Job—hearing of a problem or crisis, facing the news well, keeping my eyes focused on the Lord for the solution. But then, after some time, as I've mulled over the situation, I've found myself starting to get upset. At such times I may well be looking more at the consequences of the problem than to the Lord. Negative thoughts may run through my head. If I'm not careful, I'll open myself to favorably considering the attacks on God made by the Accuser of the Brethren, and in so doing take my eyes off God and focus on the problem, feeling more and more anger.

In Job's case, his anger was increasingly exposed as he started to feel that God was ignoring him. He began to blame God. So God sat Job down to confront him with the reality of His presence and power. God told Job in Job 38:2–3, "Who is this that darkens my counsel with words without knowledge? Brace yourself like a man; I will question you, and you shall answer me." God went on to tell Job who is in charge. Finally, after Job's anger and misplaced priorities were addressed, God restored his life to what it was in the beginning.

Jeremiah is another great example of repressed anger. Jeremiah has been labeled the "weeping prophet." He was given an incredible task with an equally incredible responsibility. Yet no one would listen to him. On one occasion Jeremiah said, "I never sat in the company of revelers, never made merry with them; I sat alone because your hand was on me and you had filled me with indignation. Why is my pain unending and my wound grievous and incurable? Will you be to me like a deceptive brook, like a spring that fails?" (Jeremiah 15:17–18).

Resentful Anger

People with resentful anger get their feelings hurt and never get over it. They hold a grudge even to the extent of getting depressed. Think how a single incident can get neighbors embroiled in a fight that causes them to be "enemies" as long as they live in the neighborhood. Family members often hold resentful anger for a lifetime. Siblings can be rivals, especially if the secondborn can never successfully compete with the older child. So much resentment can build up that the offended party may refuse to have any interaction with the other, even in adulthood.

The best example of resentful anger in the Bible is found in the parable of the Prodigal Son. The story is recorded in Luke 15:11–32. A young teenager from a good family decided to sow his wild oats. He wanted out! He asked his dad for his share of the inheritance so he could go off and cruise the streets and experience everything he felt he had been missing by living at home. Eventually he reached a state of despair. I mean he hit rock bottom. No money, living in a field of pigs, eating what they didn't want to eat. God touched his heart and he decided to go home, where his father met him out front by the gate, gave him a hug, and threw a big party to welcome him home. The older brother was ticked. "[He] became angry and refused to go in. So his father went out and pleaded with him" (v. 28). Can't you sense the resentment here? "I'm not going into that party for my low-life brother. I'm not going to validate his ungodly lifestyle. I'm fed up with this guy."

What generated his resentment? Dad's favoritism to his brother? Maybe he resented his brother's ability to "get away with murder." It could even be that he was jealous of his brother's being able to go off and do all the things *he* had wanted to do, but never had the courage to try. Whatever it was, this man demonstrated resentful anger.

Vengeful Anger

The people who choose vengeful anger are so angry they want to get even at all costs. They've experienced the adrenaline surge that accompanies revenge, and they long for the same feeling.

I went to see the movie *The Edge* not long ago. It's the story of a rich man, his wife, and some of his employees who go into the wilderness for a camera shoot and some relaxation. After some unexpected events, the rich man and two of his workers experience a plane crash and become stranded in the snow-covered mountains of the wilderness. It's not long before they make the mistake of allowing their scent to be picked up by a bear. Earlier in the movie, they had been instructed that when a bear tastes human blood, it becomes a "man-eater." This bear is a gigantic man-eater that must be destroyed for them to survive.

Some people who struggle with anger become addicted to the taste of revenge. They forget the instruction of God in Romans 12:19, "Do not take revenge, my friends, but leave room for God's wrath, for it is written: 'It is mine to avenge; I will repay,' says the Lord." They subscribe to the blasphemous philosophy of the comedian who said, "I know why God said, 'Vengeance is mine.' He knew how much fun it is and wanted all the fun for Himself."

The Pharisees provide insight into this mind-set. Our Lord was walking through a field of grain one day and used the time to instruct His disciples and the Pharisees. As the disciples walked along, they picked up some of the heads of the grain to eat. To the Pharisees this was working, and since the event took place on the Sabbath, they complained about it to Jesus. Jesus reminded them of an incident in the Old Testament when David and his companions ate some of the consecrated bread set aside for the Sabbath. Then he said to them, "The Son of Man is Lord of the Sabbath," referring to Himself (Luke 6:1–5).

Later, on another sabbath, Jesus entered a synagogue to teach. The enraged Pharisees followed Him in, tracking Him like man-eating bears anxious to trip Him up on any excuse. A man with a crippled hand was in the synagogue, and Jesus healed him, again on the Sabbath. The Pharisees said to themselves, *Gotcha!* Their anger was exposed, as Luke records. "They were furious and began to discuss with one another what they might do to Jesus" (Luke 6:11). They began to plot how to get even.

OUR PROPER RESPONSE TO ANGER

I am always looking for good advice. I realize there are many channels through which God allows good advice to come. Among the means He uses are the Bible; the Spirit's unction; and the counsel of godly friends, books, and seminars. I am prone to buying those little books at the bookstore that contain short nuggets of advice. One of my favorites is *Life's Little Instruction Book*.[5] This intriguing book gives 511 suggestions on how to live a happy and rewarding life. Here are a few of my favorites:

> #1   Compliment (at least) three people every day.
> #123 Learn to listen. Opportunity sometimes knocks very softly.
> #139 Never deprive someone of hope; it may be all he has.
> #173 Be kinder than necessary.
> #221 Don't major in minor things.
> #459 Don't use time or words carelessly. Neither can be retrieved.

Proverbs 25:28 makes a strong statement about the lack of self-control that is related to anger. "Like a city whose walls are broken down is a man who lacks self-control." What could we receive that would help us fulfill this sixth commandment to the fullest?

Admit It If You Have an Anger Problem

Job eventually came to the point of openly expressing his anger toward God. "I will not keep silent; I will speak out in the anguish of my spirit, I will complain in the bitterness of my soul" (Job 7:11). It is hard to deal with a problem you won't admit to God. In fact, He is the only resource we have for truly solving our anger problem. So admit to Him and to yourself that you have a problem with anger. If you don't *talk* it out, more than likely you're going to *take* it out.

As part of this, recognize that the problem is not necessarily the anger itself, but what you *do* with the anger. Anger is often a legitimate and natural expression of a person's emotions, the same way fear is. That is why the Bible tells us, "In your anger do not sin" (Ephesians 4:26). The question is how to do that. Here are some ways.

1. *Deal with your anger immediately.*

In Ephesians 4:26–27 we are admonished, "Do not let the sun go down while you are still angry, and do not give the devil a foothold." There are valid reasons for this. The longer anger is allowed to fester, the worse the situation becomes. It is like not medicating a cold at the first sign. The longer you wait, the less chance you have of stopping the cold from running its course. Anger left unchecked will run its course and allow the devil to get a foothold, which can even lead to a stronghold. Unchecked anger is a great danger to anyone.

In marriage, Christians should never go to bed angry. This may mean every once in a while you need to have a long night of talking, but the loss of sleep is far preferable to the loss of fellowship and the fallout that comes with unresolved anger. Healing needs to start immediately.

As part of this process we need to learn to forgive. You'll notice I didn't say *"Feel* forgiveness." I know that after angry words it can take some time for our emotions to calm down. That is human nature. But in our minds we can choose to be obedient to the Lord when

He has told us we are to forgive others because He has forgiven us (see Matthew 6:14–15; Mark 11:25–26; Luke 6:37; 17:3–4). That means we choose to give forgiveness. Our feelings may or may not correspond to that forgiveness. Eventually they should. But the important thing is to be obedient to the Lord, to forgive, and then to walk in faith that the forgiveness is a done deal, and not to walk by sight by looking at our feelings.

2. *Think before you speak.*

We need to put our minds in gear before we release the brakes on our mouths. You will avoid much anger and many apologies if you think before you speak. James 1:19–20 gives the clue as to how to accomplish this feat. "Everyone should be quick to listen, slow to speak and slow to become angry, for man's anger does not bring about the righteous life that God desires."

Remember, blowing your stack only creates air pollution. Many people are unaware that loud voices in discussions can lead to hurt and anger. The volume you use and the attitude you display will either increase or decrease the levels of anger. We are told in Colossians 3:8 to get rid of *all* anger. This is not an option but a necessity.

3. *Seek God's guidance and control.*

Your problem may look impossible. But even though with man forgiveness may seem impossible, with God nothing is impossible. A key part of controlling anger is to bring the Lord into the picture. I have always found it important at the beginning of my day to ask the Lord to put a check on my lips, to help me think before I speak, to give me the Holy Spirit's control in everything I say and do that day. I also ask Him to bring glory to Himself through me that day. When I surrender my day to Him, for His control, it is always amazing to me how much less tension or need for anger there is. Try it. It works!

In Ephesians 5:18 we are told to be filled with the Spirit of God. When we ask Him to fill us, He will. Then, when we are living our lives, filled with the Spirit of God—the very Spirit whose fruit is love, joy, peace, and patience—we will be able to start displaying this fruit in our lives, too.

Affirm Others with Thoughts and Words

Ben Franklin is said to have observed, "Speak ill of no man, but speak all the good you know of everybody." I've found that when I start thinking or speaking negative words to myself about others, or when I take the next step of allowing my mouth to verbalize such thoughts, I create an angry or at best a negative response to the person. So I make it a habit to think positive thoughts. Isn't this part of why our parents told us, "If you can't say something good about a person, don't say anything at all"?

Proverbs 25:11 puts it this way, "A word aptly spoken is like apples of gold in settings of silver." Or look at it from another biblical perspective: "A gentle answer turns away wrath" (Proverbs 15:1).

One way to be affirming, when appropriate, is to say something like, "I know I don't say this often, but . . ." As part of affirmation, you can look into a person's eyes and say, "You are valuable to me." When you do this you

- momentarily put a stop to grasping and self-asserting,
- make yourself vulnerable, and
- upset the apple cart of most relational systems.

Two factors are important for good compliments. The first is *specific content*. Rather than saying, "I sure do appreciate you," try, "You have so many wonderful qualities. I appreciate your quick smile, the way you . . ." The second is *timing*. Sometimes we want to compliment someone, but the timing is bad. A husband who wants to compliment his wife's cooking probably won't want to do so just after she has burned the meat! Nor will a father want to reward misbehavior by complimenting a child immediately after he has broken household rules.

Timing and specific content can turn a compliment into a four-course meal.

McGinnis says that part of his *Friendship Factor* is what he calls the art of affirmation. He writes,

> The art of affirmation is enhanced if we learn to express praise when it is not expected. There are certain occasions, such as after a well-prepared meal or a fine speech, when it is mere social custom to compliment. Sir Henry Taylor, in his nineteenth-century book *The Statesman*, makes the point that to wait and recall the details of an incident later will be more effective: "Applaud a man's speech at the moment when he sits down and he will take your compliment as exacted by the demands of common civility; but let some space intervene, and then show him that the merits of his speech have dwelt with you when you might have been expected to have forgotten them, and he will remember your compliment for a much longer time than you have remembered his speech."[6]

Larry Crabb, in his landmark book, *Connecting*, speaks to the concept of a "soul disease" innate to all of us and then addresses a means of helping and healing one another through "connecting." He writes:

Ordinary people have the power to change other people's lives. An older priest can revitalize a despairing younger colleague by pulling the troubled man's head to his chest. A distraught father can touch his son with an energy that cuts through a hardened heart and awakens what is tender and true within the child. An adult daughter can offer something from hidden places within her to her aging mother that releases hope in the elderly woman's heart, hope that can support her through her loneliness, confusion, and pain.[7]

We have the power to change lives, motivate discouraged souls, and encourage downtrodden people. It's the power of the Holy Spirit at work within us when we tap into this often unused resource. We can become the loving extension of God's hands to encourage and heal as we compliment.

How I identify with Mark Twain when he said, "I can live two months on one good compliment." Let's get practical again. You have a chance to apply this right now as you read. What are some ways you can compliment people this week?

1. *Write postcards or notes.*

You can jot a word of encouragement to someone who needs it, even someone with whom you have not always been in harmony.

2. *Pray for the person.*

It is hard to be angry at someone you are praying for. Claim Scripture for the person as you pray—Scripture that will build the person up, not be used as a weapon against him.

Restore Broken Relationships

This is the target. We have all experienced the pain of broken relationships. Let me give you a few pointers that may help if you have hurt somebody or been hurt by another and you seek reconciliation.

1. *Have pure motives.*

Reconciliation will only happen when your motives are right. If you are trying to reconcile for self-gratification, to see the other person grovel, or to prove you are right, then you will never have true reconciliation. You will be building on the wrong foundation.

2. *Have a humble approach.*

Arrogance is a dead end. Arrogance says to the person, "Don't tell me. . . . I know!" Humility can lead to reconciliation. Humility gives the other person the benefit of the doubt. In essence it asks, "What was your perspective?" Proverbs 18:2 reminds us, "A fool finds no pleasure in understanding but delights in airing his own opinions."

3. *Take time for prayer with the person, if he is a believer.*

This will help to break down walls and will be instrumental in a healthy approach to confrontation and reconciliation. Whenever we bring the Lord into our problems, He can smooth the situation out and help restore health to the relationship.

CONCLUSION

Every person gets angry, but dealing with anger in a constructive way is a part of God's Top Ten List. And when we take to heart what we learn from this sixth principle, it's amazing how much less pressure and how much more joy we experience. After all, will getting as angry as you do make any sense when you get to the end of your life?

When I speak to leaders across North America, I constantly challenge them to look *forward* and then look back. I ask them to take a giant mental step forward to near the end of their life and then think back to what seems significant from that perspective. You can do the same. Imagine: You have survived life's many seasons; you have endured life's mountaintop experiences and valleys of pain. Will you really remember how angry you were at the post office because there were never enough people working the counter? Do you really think a major point of discussion in your rocking chair will be the neighbors' noise levels when you were trying to sleep in? Will you sit and make a long list of those things that just ticked you off and rate them on a level on "tickedness"? (If there is such a word!) Was all that "stuff" worth losing a friendship over or causing such pain in your home or dividing your church?

Never forget, there comes a time when God calls all His children home. If you are a Christian, you have a tremendous hope awaiting you in heaven. When you die, the shell, your body, will be placed in the ground and a nice headstone will be put on your grave telling others the date you were born, a dash, and the date you died. What will matter will not be the date you were born or the date God says, "You're done! Come on home." What will have mattered is what you have done with your "dash." Dealing with your anger may give you both a longer dash and a more fulfilling dash. You get to choose. I have given some suggestions below of ways to deal with your anger.

TOP TEN WAYS
TO DEAL WITH YOUR ANGER

1. *Begin or renew a great relationship with God!*

2. *Tell someone how much he or she matters to you—and be specific.*

3. *Never go to bed angry.*

4. *Take the first step toward restoring a broken relationship.*

5. *Send up a prayer.*

6. *Memorize James 1:19.*

7. *Count to ten if you're angry and a hundred if really "ticked."*

8. *Look for creative ways to compliment someone who really bothers you. This can include doing something nice for that person, giving the person a gift, and praying positively for that person.*

9. *Brainstorm ways to help the less fortunate in your community.*

10. *Write a card to encourage someone.*

Notes

1. Stephen May, *Sermon Notes* 4, no. 2 (issue 21): 33.
2. Alan Loy McGinnis, *The Friendship Factor* (Minneapolis: Augsburg, 1979), 99.
3. Dean Ornish, quoted in Redford Williams and Virginia Williams, *Anger Kills* (New York: Harper Perennial, 1984).
4. Ibid., 58–59.
5. H. Jackson Brown, Jr., *Life's Little Instruction Book* (Nashville: Rutledge Hill, 1991).
6. McGinnis, *Friendship Factor,* 98.
7. Larry Crabb, *Connecting* (Nashville: Word, 1997), 31.

chapter eight

Affair-Proofing Your Marriage

"You shall not commit adultery."

—Exodus 20:14

It shouldn't come as a shock for me to tell you that half of all marriages end in divorce. At one time it was the "seven-year itch," but now it's the "five-year rash" that enters the relationship, and the husband or wife decides, for whatever reason, that he or she married the wrong person. That partner walks out . . . or has an affair. Nancy and I have been married more than twenty-four years. In this time, we have seen many people walk away from their families, their mates, and their stability. They may have entered the airplane of marriage excited about the ride and ready for the long journey, but they have always worn a parachute "just in case." And when turbulence hits, they jump.

How do you affair-proof a marriage? This must be very important, because it's a part of God's Top Ten List: "You shall not commit adultery" (Exodus 20:14). Probably the greatest reason so many struggle in this area is that people do not understand the needs of their mates and how to meet them.

THE TOP TEN NEEDS OF
MEN AND WOMEN IN A RELATIONSHIP

According to Willard Harley, in *His Needs, Her Needs,*[1] we all bring basic needs to a relationship. All of those needs are important. Yet, not surprisingly, men's and women's needs often differ significantly. I have categorized Dr. Harley's top ten list into two columns to enable you to see the differences between the man's point of view and the woman's point of view.

Her Needs:	His Needs:
1. Affection	1. Sexual fulfillment
2. Conversation	2. Recreation
3. Honesty and openness	3. Attractiveness
4. Financial support	4. Domestic support
5. Family commitment	5. Admiration

The premise of Harley's book rests upon an understanding that our needs as men and women are different, even if we don't realize the differences. And it's in those unmet needs that we find the greatest temptations to affairs. But when the needs are met, the chances for an affair are greatly diminished. Harley's developed his list of top ten needs after many years of counseling. The lists below expand Harley's definitions.

Needs of Women

1. Affection: "I need you to *express your feelings for me* in small ways."
2. Conversation: "I need you to *talk* to me."

3. Honesty and Openness: "I need to *know what's going on* in your life."
4. Financial Support: "I need you to *provide* enough for us to live comfortably."
5. Family Commitment: "I need you to *be a family person.*"

Needs of Men

1. Sexual Fulfillment: "I need you to have *sex* with me."
2. Recreational Companionship: "I need to *play and have fun* together."
3. Attractiveness: "I need you to *look good.*"
4. Domestic Support: "I need you to *take care of the home front.*"
5. Admiration: "I need you to *be proud of me.*"

Looking at the chronology of these lists, I want you to notice three things. (1) Whereas a man *desires* domestic support, a woman *fears for* financial support. I sense we are seeing some shift in this thinking, however, as women become more common in the workplace. (2) A man's number two need is *recreation,* whereas a woman's is *conversation.* A man tends to feel close while *doing* something, but a woman views intimacy as *saying* something. (3) If a wife doesn't receive *affection and tenderness,* she is less likely to respond *sexually.* And if the husband doesn't receive *sex,* it's much more difficult to show *tenderness and affection.* So tenderness and affection are in a round-robin with sex. Sexuality couched in affection can contribute greatly to the health of a relationship, but the absence of sexuality in a marriage can give a spouse an excuse to find sexual expression outside the marriage. Maybe this is why God gives us the seventh commandment in such absolute terms: "You *shall not* commit adultery."

GOD'S STANDARD: SEXUAL PURITY

God's standard for our culture is not flexible—He wants 100 percent sexual purity. That does not mean we should refrain from sexual activity or suppress all sexual thoughts. Nor does it mean that sex by nature is something dirty we should hide, or that it's something somehow "impolite." God created sex to be a good thing. In fact, from all we know of anatomy, He created it to be *great!* But it does mean that we are to express sexuality within the arena God designed: marital relationship.

God's commandment about purity has two elements. The first element is the physical one. We are to save sexual activity for our spouse. The commandment from God is clear, terse, absolute: "No adultery!" A man must not engage in sexual activity with anyone other than his wife, and a woman must not engage in sexual activity with anyone other than her husband. This is the physical side of understanding God's decree.

The second element is the emotional and mental side of the commandment. We are to save sexual thoughts for our mates. In the last chapter we saw what Jesus did to the command "You shall not murder." He carried it to its logical conclusion. It's not just about killing people. It's about what's going on in your heart in dealing with your anger. Jesus does the same thing when he talks about adultery. Matthew 5:27–30 states:

> "You have heard that it was said, 'Do not commit adultery.' But I tell you that anyone who looks at a woman lustfully has already committed adultery with her in his heart. If your right eye causes you to sin, gouge it out and throw it away. It is better for you to lose one part of your

body than for your whole body to be thrown into hell. And if your right hand causes you to sin, cut it off and throw it away. It is better for you to lose one part of your body than for your whole body to go into hell."

Whoa! Does this say what I think it says? A whole lot of adultery is going on! This means that there are thousands of people all over America committing adultery with *Sports Illustrated* swimsuit editions and *Victoria's Secret* catalogs. Thousands of people are committing adultery with Miss May—and Mr. May—at magazine stands and bookstores. Others are committing adultery with fictitious characters in romance novels and soap operas in quiet homes every day. People commit adultery every day with coworkers, friends, and neighbors, even though they may have never touched each other.

Why does God call this adultery? Why is Jesus so extreme? So adamant about something so apparently innocent? He calls this adultery because adultery, like murder, begins in the heart. God is no killjoy or a prude. He doesn't want to cramp our style or limit our fun. Remember: God *created* sex. (Would a prude—would *you*—have thought of it?) You matter deeply to Him. When God sets a standard, He has a very good reason for it. Adultery involves the whole person, mind and body, and it begins in the thoughts of our heart. Jesus was using extreme language, even hyperbole, to make the point so strong we can't ignore it.

There's another reason God so strongly condemns the adultery that has gone only so far as our thoughts. Adultery of the heart is a betrayal. It rips away promises you have made, puts a barrier of lies between you and your spouse, and causes your spouse deep pain. Adultery cannot be a way of expressing your love for your spouse.

GOD'S REASON FOR SEXUAL PURITY

I believe there are distinct reasons for God's desiring us to have personal purity. First, He wants us to have *wholeness*, to enjoy physical, emotional, and spiritual well-being. Proverbs 6:32 says, "But a man who commits adultery lacks judgment; whoever does so destroys himself." We are physical, emotional, and spiritual beings. Marriage is the physical, emotional, and spiritual union of two people. The Bible says in Genesis 2:24, "For this reason a man will leave his father and mother and be united to his wife, and they will become one flesh." Willard Harley says, "With exclusivity comes responsibility. If you fail to meet your spouse's need for, say, recreational companionship, he or she can find that elsewhere. But, if you expect your spouse to be your exclusive sex partner, you have a special responsibility to meet your spouse's sexual needs."[2]

Now this doesn't mean that just because your spouse isn't meeting your needs you are excused from the requirement not to commit adultery. It just says how dangerous it is to fail to address the genuine concerns of your spouse.

Sex is not just a union of bodies but also a union of souls. This is the realm (physical, emotional, spiritual commitment) for sex. Sex becomes the ultimate act of relational intimacy for beings who were created for relationships. Ripped from that context and made into something purely physical, we make the act less human, and we degrade ourselves into something less than human. Too often we start behaving as animals without restraint. In the process, we also degrade and devalue others.

Lust is the devaluing of a person. It lowers another

person to the status of a thing, someone to be used for pleasure. Failing to recognize this mind-set is an affront to God and an insult to God as our Creator.

Second, God is concerned for *others'* wholeness. Sexual impurity always has relational consequences and affects others. Consider the consequences of a person's affair. Tremendous havoc and destruction lay in the wake of this person's actions. If there are children, the pain and impact is enormous. Is it worth the risk? Is sin so tantalizing that it is worth destroying everything else? Let's get back to basics for a moment.

TOP TEN REASONS
TO AVOID AN AFFAIR

1. *You will bring immeasurable pain and devastation to your children and set a bad example for them. It's hard to overestimate the trust children place in parents. Your integrity forms part of the foundation for their personal security.*

2. *You may destroy your opportunity to bring others to a healthy relationship with God. Family, friends, neighbors—anyone you may desire to bring to God—loses respect for you, especially in spiritual matters.*

3. *You will introduce into your and your spouse's life the possibility of sexually transmitted diseases. This is miserable and a great guilt-producer for you as well as a source of resentment for your spouse.*

4. *You will damage God's relationship with your partner in the affair. If the other person is a believer, you may be pulling him or her away from God. If not, you may be significantly harming his or her likelihood of coming to Christ for salvation. Your actions may have eternal consequences!*

5. *You will degrade and harm your partner in the affair. Your partner will feel violated, inadequate, and rejected.*

6. *You will bring disgrace to God's name and reputation. If you are a believer, people who know you relate your actions to God either positively or negatively.*

7. *Your conscience will be forever seared. You will never be able to forget it and will struggle with accepting the forgiveness of God and your spouse.*

8. *You will destroy trust and integrity in all your relationships. You will no longer be considered a model of integrity by anyone who knows you.*

9. *You will do permanent harm to your spouse and your relationship with him or her. A marriage devastated by adultery may end in divorce, though it doesn't have to. Yet the aftermath of adultery will never really go away. Trust and integrity will remain issues in your marriage.*

10. *Your relationship with God will be damaged. Though He will love you and forgive you, your relationship with God will suffer damage. You will feel guilty, and it will be hard for you to experience intimacy with God.*

We must never forget that sexual purity has relational consequences. Let's look at a biblical example. God's concern for the wholeness of others is illustrated in 1 Thessalonians 4:3–7:

It is God's will that you should be sanctified: that you should avoid sexual immorality; that each of you should learn to control his own body in a way that is holy and honorable, not in passionate lust like the heathen, who do not know God; and that in this matter no one should wrong his brother or take advantage of him. The Lord will punish men for all such sins, as we have already told you and warned you. For God did not call us to be impure, but to live a holy life.

This is so important that Paul includes a warning: "The Lord will punish." Paul wants his readers to know there are divine consequences to sexual impurity. But Paul doesn't end on a note of warning. Faith is a much better motivator than fear. So Paul reminds them of their purpose, their *calling*. God has a destiny for you, a call on your life, and He wants to work through you to change His world. Your purpose in life is not to be impure, destroying self and others, but to live a holy life— unique, dedicated to God, and full of integrity.

OUR RESPONSE:
GUARDING SEXUAL PURITY

"OK, Lord, we get the idea. This is obviously a big deal in Your eyes. How should I respond?" This is the cry of a person who is seeking God's heart. It is high time that we start allowing the things that break God's heart to break ours, and personal purity is one of His Top Ten. So let's look at some practical ways to affair-proof your marriage, whether you are presently married or hope that marriage is a part of God's plan on your horizon. (And this also means that you should guard your purity even if you stay single!)

Make a Commitment to God's Standard

Look again at 1 Thessalonians 4:7, "For God did not call us to be impure, but to live a holy life." Make a commitment to live the life that God has called you to. If married, choose to make a commitment today to God's standard: sexual purity. Make that commitment *public and obvious*. ("I'm unavailable.") Let your spouse know you are committed to this relationship and will never wear a parachute "just in case" you want to bail out.

But what if you are single? One word: *Abstinence.* This may seem completely anachronistic, archaic, or even prudish. "Come on, Glen, this is simply unrealistic. How will we know if we're compatible if we don't live together? Would you buy a shoe without trying it on?" This is false reasoning. Research has shown that those who cohabit before marriage have a higher chance of divorce than those who don't.[3] The notion that cohabitation before marriage is good for marriage is simply a temptation of the devil.

- Neil Anderson and Charles Mylander note, "This is earth, not heaven. It is a fallen world, not an ideal one. Every Christian must watch out for 'that ancient serpent, who is the devil or Satan'" (Revelation 20:2). It's not by accident that the Bible calls Satan a serpent. He is as venomous as a rattlesnake."[4] We know that poisonous snakes may inflict deadly snakebites; we know that when we experience a bite, a snake was involved and so we flee snakes. But when we receive a moral "bite," we sometimes forget that a "snake" is behind that too and so forget to flee the snake.
- Pornography is not the snake, but the snakebite.
- Abortion is not the snake, but the snakebite.
- Adultery is not the snake, but its lethal poison.[5]

Make a commitment to God's standard. Make a commitment to His calling on your life, His destiny for you.

"Yeah, but Glen, I've already blown it! I realize the effect upon my home. I have felt the pain, the guilt, and the inner turmoil. What do I do?" You may be married and now suffering the devastating effects of affairs you have had in the past. You may be married and well on your way to or already engaged in an affair right now. You find yourself locked into an emotional affair: flirting, talking. Maybe you're single and in a relationship you know is less than God's ideal for you. What do you do?

First, *own up to it*. Take responsibility; confess it to God and to others. First John 1:9 says, "If we confess our sins, he is faithful and just and will forgive us our sins and purify us from all unrighteousness."

Second, *receive and give forgiveness*. Forgiveness is a choice.

Probably the best piece of advice I can give you is the third point. *Begin again*. Immediately change your behavior. But you cannot do this successfully by yourself. You need the help of the Holy Spirit. The Lord says in Philippians 4:13 that we can do all things through Jesus who gives us strength. Not our own strength, but His. So you need to confess your weakness to avoid sexual temptation. Tell Him that you know He wants you to live purely, so if you ever are going to be able to, He has to intervene. Then ask Him to give you His strength each day to live the right way, to resist temptation, to avoid sin. You can start anew today. Simply pray and ask Him to take control of every area of your life. And then, by God's grace and with the help of His community, today you can make a commitment to His standard of sexual purity.

Maximize Your Marriage

A growing relationship with your spouse reduces the attraction of an affair. We are reminded in Ephesians

5:33, "However, each one of you also must love his wife as he loves himself, and the wife must respect her husband." In Ephesians 5, Paul tells husbands to love their wives by sacrificing themselves for them just as Christ gave Himself for us—by putting their wives' needs before their own. Paul then, in turn, tells wives to respond by meeting their husbands' needs.

If we go back to Harley's original top ten list, we find that when those needs go unmet, spouses become susceptible to an affair. How? Needs may go unmet, but they do not go away. Along comes someone who "appreciates" you and talks to you. You're stimulated (naturally —a need is met) and often without your even thinking through the process, the situation adds to your underlying resentment against your spouse for not meeting your needs. The fuel has been added to the sticks you have gathered, and it only takes a tiny match to set them ablaze.

Now, again, I'm not saying that simply having a need excuses you from taking the shortcut to fill it. Nor am I saying that because you have a need you are owed whatever it is that would fill it. You can't say, "If I'm thirsty, it's OK for me to drink." What I am saying is that Harley's secret to affair-proofing your marriage *works*. Become *aware* of each other's needs and *learn to meet them*. "Make your grass so green that everyone else's lawn looks brown by comparison." Remember, the grass is greenest where it is watered. So focus your attention, your nurturing, on your spouse's needs. Become such an incredible lover and partner that your spouse would have to be an idiot to go elsewhere.

God has given you a wonderful mate, handpicked just for you. Will there be times when this person is divine sandpaper in your life? Of course! That's part of

God's plan. You don't want to remain with rough edges, do you?

One of the best pieces of advice I could give you is to join a couples' group in your church. We weren't intended to go at this thing alone! People all around you have traveled this road and faced your struggles. Stop the negative thinking and gather a support network around you of fellow believers who will pray for you. Instead of always looking at your own selfish needs, tell God and your mate, "If my spouse is going to have a good lover, it's going to be me. I choose this day to take off my parachute."

Stop and think for a minute. If you are committed to fulfilling your spouse's needs and your spouse is committed to fulfilling yours, instead of doing this for yourselves in a self-centered way, won't you both win as you each get your needs fulfilled by the other? Truly looking out for the interests of your mate is a win-win situation. Your mate wins and so do you.

Minimize the Opportunities

The Bible is very clear on this subject. Paul wrote in 1 Corinthians 6:18, "Flee from sexual immorality. All other sins a man commits are outside his body, but he who sins sexually sins against his own body." He likewise admonished a young pastor named Timothy in 2 Timothy 2:22, "Flee the evil desires of youth, and pursue righteousness, faith, love and peace, along with those who call on the Lord out of a pure heart." God says, *Run!* He doesn't say, "Flirt with temptation." He doesn't say, "See how close you can get to the flames without getting burned." God says, "Get out of there. Run like the wind."

A great biblical example would be Joseph. Joseph's

life had not been a bed of roses. He came from a dys-
functional family, had lost a major power struggle with
his brothers, and surely could be understood if he had
doubted God's hand's being in control throughout the
turmoil. His boss's wife, Mrs. Potiphar, decided that
Joseph was cute and made a move on him. Joseph resis-
ted the temptation over and over, but this only frustrated her. Finally, she became more aggressive, and the
only option left to Joseph was to run. He got out of there
so abruptly that he even left behind his favorite jacket.

Sometimes, you will need to leave your jacket behind—just *run!* This is not about exercising self-control.
It's about not finding yourself in a place where you will
need self-control. Don't stand in front of the magazine
rack—nor even go into the stores. Tear up your card to
that video store with the adult section. Call ahead on
business trips to have adult pay TV channels canceled.
Call the phone company and have 900 numbers blocked.
Disconnect the Internet if this becomes an area of compromise in your life. If you travel a lot, develop a pact or
agreement with a friend or spouse. I have two men who
ask me the tough questions after a trip. "What kind of
movies did you watch? Did you do anything that would
affect your intimacy with your family and with God?"
Then they always ask me the toughest question: "Did
you just lie to me?"

All of us must maintain appropriate relationships
with members of the opposite sex and keep appropriate
limits as to how long a touch or a glance should last. I
am a hugger, so I hug when appropriate. But I don't
overdo it. Beyond that, I find most touching should be
avoided. Avoid alone-time (luncheons, meetings) with
members of the opposite sex.

Another important safeguard is to keep good company.

Are your best friends as committed to their marriages as you? First Corinthians 15:33 reminds us, "Do not be misled: 'Bad company corrupts good character.'" It is easy to let our standards slip when we are around those whose standards are below ours.

If you are single, note again Paul's advice to Timothy. God doesn't want you to repress sexual energy, and God doesn't want you to release sexual energy illegitimately. He calls you to *rechannel* sexual energy. "*Flee* the evil desires of youth, and *pursue* righteousness, faith, love and peace, along with those who call on the Lord out of a pure heart" (2 Timothy 2:22, italics added). Pour yourself into serving God, knowing and loving God, and being used by God to affect your community and the world. If you do, God promises to take care of you. Matthew 6:33 verifies this truth: "But seek first his kingdom and his righteousness, and all these things will be given to you as well."

CONCLUSION

Monogamy works! God says so. This is not an abnormal way to live. It's the normal and expected way. Monogamy isn't even dull. Opening your heart to someone else and being completely vulnerable to someone who loves you and is sacrificing for you opens you up to know and be known, to love and be loved. I tell people in my church that there would be far fewer marriages in court if there were more courting in our marriages. Could that be the answer to living "happily ever after"?

The key is to change your mind. When you change your thinking, your life will change. We cannot blame our sin on anyone but us. Sin is but the result of internal desires that we give in to. James 4:1 says, "What causes fights and quarrels among you? Don't they come from *your desires* that battle within you?" (italics added). Take responsibility today. Don't claim to be a part of this victimized society. David could have said: "It was Bathsheba's fault—look what she was wearing at the time." Or he could have even blamed God. "Lord, You could have prevented her from bathing where I could see her. . . . You caused this in my life." God will never say no in His Word and yes to your feelings. When David stopped and reflected that it was time to take responsibility for his actions, he proclaimed in Psalm 51:4, "Against you [God], you only, have I sinned and done what is evil in your sight."

Joseph, unlike David, took responsibility and fled. He did not give in nor allow himself the excuse, "I am not responsible. I am a slave and have to do what my master and mistress ask of me." He followed God's way and in the long run was greatly blessed. He never would have become second in command in Egypt if he had not been thrown into jail. God will reward our faithfulness to Him and His standards.

Marriage is a lot like a great river flowing downstream. You are enjoying the ride and the scenery on a tributary when all of a sudden your tributary merges with another, or in some cases, collides. You get married. Now there is white water. The ride is a little tougher and sometimes not so enjoyable. But as the river moves downstream a little farther, the river again calms and the ride is smoother. Marriage takes commitment to the journey and commitment to the future. Will there be future white water? Probably! When a child comes along, the ride gets rougher. You move . . . hold on. You change jobs; you face times of insecurity. The key is this: Hold on! But be certain it is God to whom you hold.

Notes

1. Willard Harley, *His Needs, Her Needs* (Grand Rapids: Revell, 1996).
2. Willard F. Harley, *Give and Take: The Secret to Marital Compatibility* (Grand Rapids: Revell, 1996), 187.
3. "The Relationship Between Cohabitation and Divorce," *Demography,* 1992.
4. Neil T. Anderson and Charles Mylander, *The Christ-Centered Marriage* (Ventura, Calif.: Regal, 1996), 201–2.
5. Ibid.

chapter nine

Managing Money Honestly

"You shall not steal."

—Exodus 20:15

We'd all like not to be affected by stealing. But it affects all of us. Banks are hit and millions are lost in shoplifting each year, with the result of higher prices and higher insurance premiums for everybody. Wouldn't it be nice if we didn't have to worry about theft? If we lived in a society where we didn't have to lock our doors? That's the kind of society God was trying to set up with the Jews. Again, we see God's perfect plan as demonstrated in God's Top Ten. You aren't going to get any clearer than the eighth principle in our study together, Exodus 20:4, "You shall not steal." In fact the Hebrew really only has two words, "Not steal!" It's pretty straightforward, isn't it?

HOW DO WE STEAL?

Stealing is more than simply breaking into a bank or someone's home, or taking someone's wallet. There are 138 synonyms for the word *steal* in the thesaurus, each with a slightly different meaning. We can't look at them all, but let's just look at some of the ones that start with "D."

1. *Deceiving customers.*

Withholding important information about a used item, scheduling unnecessary repairs or tests, using deceitful descriptions are all a part of the word *stealing.* You get ready to sell your used car, and a relative says that the car has too many miles for its age. He suggests you let him roll the odometer back to fifty thousand miles. That's stealing.

2. *Deluding employers.*

We are stealing when we delude employers into thinking that we're doing a good job, but we are actually taking extralong coffee and lunch breaks; making lots of personal phone calls; and taking home pens, staplers, and other office supplies. That's stealing.

3. *Delaying payments.*

This is the idea of wanting our money back right away but taking forever to pay back those we owe. In business you would bill others at thirty days but take up to ninety days to pay your own bills. You're keeping the money longer so you can earn interest on it.

4. *Defaulting on loans.*

This is where we borrow with the full intention of not giving it back. Or we borrow with the intention of paying it back but then not getting around to actually doing it. This happens way too often with personal loans to and from friends. It's not just money either. Sometimes we borrow items and forget to give them back. In our minds, the property gradually becomes ours. I wonder how many books I have lost from my library because of this category of theft.

5. *Duping the government.*

Legal tax deductions are good stewardship of our money, but tax evasion is illegal. In many of our minds the fine line between these two is too easily crossed over. It could be income that's not reported, a deduction that you really don't qualify for, or something else.

6. *Defrauding God.*

We can cheat God by not giving Him what He is due. Jesus said, "Give to Caesar what is Caesar's, and to God what is God's" (Matthew 22:21). And what is God's? Everything. All that we have He has given us. All that He asks in return is 10 percent. That's less than the government wants! He also wants us to love Him with our whole being. Anything less is cheating God, or stealing from Him.

WHY SHOULD I BE HONEST?

I appreciate the words of Michael Hodgin:

In the study of logic, there is one significant difference between a valid argument and a sound argument: the truth! Both arguments may have conclusions that consistently follow from the premises of the arguments. But a valid argument does not have to contain premises—or assumptions—that are true. In ancient Greece, philosophers called sophists could take either side of an argument and present a logical conclusion. These ancient sophists—similar to many modern-day lawyers—took less pride in knowing the truth [than] they did in knowing how to win debates.[1]

Yet the secular thinking of today demands we give a logical defense of our stand for the right. So, why should we be honest?

We Are Being Watched

Luther E. Smith is professor of church and community at Emory University's Candler School of Theology. He had this to say in a speech to students about living honestly: "Faking it for a class session is one thing. But it is so easy to find ourselves making faking it a lifestyle. We fake it with others. We fake it with ourselves. We fake it with God. This summer I saw a bumper sticker that said: 'Jesus is coming. Look busy!'"[2]

The Bible says in Job 34:21–22, "His eyes are on the ways of men; he sees their every step. There is no dark place, no deep shadow, where evildoers can hide." Sometimes we do things we think no one will ever know about. But God sees all that we do. There is no hiding from Him, and there is no escaping His justice. There will be an accounting. Also, your family watches you. They know the real you. The "Do as I say, not as I do" routine just doesn't cut it. Much of what we are will be passed on to our children. They will catch it without ever realizing it.

We Will Reap What We Sow

Galatians 6:7 speaks very clearly to this issue. "Do not be deceived: God cannot be mocked. A man reaps what he sows." As you treat others so shall you be treated. It's the way things work. Sooner or later, justice is served.

Again, the life of Joseph demonstrates this truth. His brothers thought they would never be discovered for selling him to the caravans that took him to Egypt. Yet in the end, everyone learned about it, including their father and all who read the account in Genesis. The biblical account lets us know that decades after their evil act, their consciences were still bothering them, for they tied their current problems with getting food into the sin committed so long ago against Joseph. At one point, they bowed down before their despised brother, begging for his mercy—the same mercy they had withheld from him as he begged them not to sell him into slavery.

Dishonesty Damages Our Character

Luke 16:10 says, "Whoever can be trusted with very little can also be trusted with much, and whoever is dishonest with very little will also be dishonest with much." That's the basic test of integrity. It starts with the "little things." The little things naturally lead to the big things. Ask any police officer. If you become known as a dishonest person (even if everyone else is doing it!), people will feel that they can't trust you. Trust is difficult to earn and even harder to re-earn.

Think of the hypothetical situation where your neighbor has nothing good to say about the rest of his neighbors. He constantly complains to you about Joe, Frank, and Mr. Bolts down the street. Yet you know he has never said these things to their faces. If you are like me, such behavior makes you wonder what he says about you when you're not around. Frankly speaking, such a neighbor would have a hard time *ever* having my confidence unless he came to me, admitted his negative attitude, and said he no longer wanted to be this way and was going to do everything he could to speak only edifying words about people. In such a case, and especially if he was a believer and was asking for God's help, I would be able to trust him much sooner. Time would show if he succeeded or not.

Another way you can damage your character is by stealing small things from the company you work for. When others know of this, they will look down on you, even if they do it themselves. In part this may be because you are a believer and they know believers are not supposed to steal from others. However, a more embarrassing consequence kicks in if you are discovered by management. Then you may well get fired and, if so, you will not get a good reference for your next job, making it much harder to get a decent-paying job. In such a situation, you are risking a lot to be dishonest.

You may start out with paper clips, but my experience as a pastor who counsels people in similar situations shows you might well start stealing more and more valuable things as you ignore your conscience, which God designed as a protection against yielding to sin.

God Will Reward Honesty

Solomon said in Proverbs 28:20, "A faithful man will be richly blessed, but one eager to get rich will not go unpunished." If you are faithful and honest, you will be rewarded. That God will reward honesty is a tremendous motivation for continued honesty.

As much as we may bad-mouth big business these days, the one admirable thing the top fifty most profitable corporations have in common is a moral code of ethics. They couldn't last in business any other way. They've discovered what God knew all the time: Honesty is the best policy. You cannot truly succeed in the long run without it.

Isn't it wonderful that God has given us these Top Ten Principles that, if followed, would put us way ahead of those who do not follow them or who have to learn them the hard way?

MOTIVATIONS FOR DISHONESTY

After examining typical motivations toward honesty as a lifestyle, we remain aware that there are many other motivations for dishonesty. Let's not be blindsided by Satan's allurement toward this kind of life. What are some of these motivations?

Greed

Greed is desiring something that doesn't belong to you. It also applies to wanting something for nothing, or next to nothing. It speaks about not being willing to work for something. I came across a sad but true story about a pastor from Georgia. In February of 1997, the Reverend Duane B. Partin was deep in debt to his parishioners. He walked into the woods in southern Laurens County near Irwinton, Georgia, wrote a suicide message on his shirt, and killed himself. Thirty-three people, most of them from the three or four churches he served, filed a lawsuit against his estate, claiming that Partin—who was not a licensed securities dealer, investment adviser, or financial planner—had persuaded them to sink a total of $2.1 million into investments he told them were good ones even though he had every reason to know they were not.

The Irwinton attorney who filled the lawsuit commented, "That's really the heartbreaking part of this case. You had a minister who used his spiritual influence to induce people to part with their money." Then the lawyer said this, "Carrying a Bible and a promissory note at the same time is not a good mixture."[3]

Matthew 6:24 is just as true today as it was when our Lord spoke it: "No one can serve two masters. Either he will hate the one and love the other, or he will be devoted to the one and despise the other. You cannot serve both God and Money." This pastor was an example of that truth. The Enemy of our souls knows that money can be a snare for anyone. Thus the strong warning from the Lord in this passage.

Laziness

Laziness is not living up to the potential God has put into you. It is looking for the shortcut, the get-rich-quick plan. People in this camp are the easiest to con. It really is true that if something seems too good to be true, it is. The wise individual knows that gaining wealth takes time; investing in mutual funds does not give you overnight wealth. You invest for the long haul.

Pride

Pride can be positive or negative, depending on your motivation. Self-satisfied pride in your own abilities and believing you are better than others are not God's way. However, He does want you to have honest self-respect and take pride in your work, to care about how it is done.

Some have the unhealthy pride that makes them feel good to "work" the other person. It's one thing to take pride in always working out a fair deal; it's another to take pride in exploiting others' weaknesses to get an unfair deal.

"You can't find an honest man who cheats." That's because an honest man isn't motivated by greed, laziness, or pride. So he won't con you. There are no weaknesses he will try to exploit.

HOW TO MANAGE YOUR MONEY WISELY

Most people do not have the luxury of having a financial planner or adviser on retainer. But did you know that one of the most successful businessmen of all time has given you some free advice in a book of wise sayings you can use to guide you financially? He was not only the world's wealthiest man, but he was also the world's wisest man. His name was Solomon, and he gave us suggestions for financial management in the Bible in the book of Proverbs. Let's examine his financial wisdom.

Keep Track of Where Your Money Is Going

I wonder how many people have said, "Wow! Where did all my money go?" Solomon said, "Be sure you know the condition of your flocks, give careful attention to your herds; for riches do not endure forever, and a crown is not secure for all generations" (Proverbs 27:23–24). Now, granted, Solomon was talking to a bunch of shepherds, and their investment was their sheep. If they kept track of their flocks, their records were intact.

But our application is clear. Basically what he's saying is pay close attention to your resources. One of the greatest reasons we get under pressure with finances is that we don't know where our money goes. Proverbs 23:23 says, "Buy the truth and do not sell it; get wisdom, discipline and understanding." In other words, get the facts at any price. Many Americans charge the things they think they need, believing (hoping) the money will be there at the end of the month. You need to keep good records. All the time you spend worrying about your finances could be invested so much more wisely if you kept good track of your money.

God is under no obligation to make us rich, but there are cases where following God's principles regarding our money results in financial reward. Recently I heard a pastor friend relate the story of counseling one of the men in his congregation who was $30,000 in debt to make a plan to pay off the debt, and at the same time to tithe 10 percent and put 10 percent into savings. It took the man three years to pay off the debt. He came back to my friend to say that he had $100,000 in cash and stocks and bonds just a few years after such heavy debt.

Pray and Plan Before You Buy

Solomon said in Proverbs 21:5, "The plans of the diligent lead to profit as surely as haste leads to poverty." Plans lead to what? Profit. As surely as haste leads to what? Poverty. Do you know what he's talking about when he speaks of haste? Impulse buying. Consider praying for it before you go paying for it. Prayer becomes a tremendous opportunity for God to change our plans or confirm them. A wise pastor pointed out to me years ago that every time I put something on my credit card I just might be lacking the faith that God will provide. I may well be failing to believe and plan on the sovereignty of God. Is it possible that many people have never seen God work in their finances because they've never prayed about them?

Have you ever wondered why you even have to ask? Because John 16:24 says, "Until now you have not asked for anything in my name. Ask and you will receive, and your joy will be complete." God wants to answer your prayers so that you will experience the joy of the Lord. It is just too easy today to shortchange God's power with credit. There is no such thing as an "easy" payment. Payments are always hard. Debt is every much an addiction as drugs and alcohol.

Again, let's look at the words of Solomon. Proverbs 21:20 says, "In the house of the wise are stores of choice food and oil, but a foolish man devours all he has." You will only get back under control by keeping track of where your money is going and by spending less than you earn.

Practice Contentment

We will be discussing this aspect of God's Top Ten List in greater detail in chapter 11. But Solomon is clear here. Proverbs 15:16–17 says, "Better a little with the fear of the Lord than great wealth with turmoil. Better a meal of vegetables where there is love than a fattened calf with hatred." Sometimes we get so busy getting more that we don't enjoy what we have. At some point this year, every American will violate this principle. "I wish I had their car, their house, their kids, their job . . ." You try to keep up with the neighbors, and they're trying to keep ahead of you.

So what happens? You get under pressure and don't enjoy today, all because you violated one of God's Top Ten.

Become a Giver

Proverbs tells us in chapter 11:24–25, "One man gives freely, yet gains even more; another withholds unduly, but comes to poverty. A generous man will prosper; he who refreshes others will himself be refreshed." What's he saying? When you share with others, God shares with you. That's the opposite of the world's wisdom. The world says, "Get everything you can, and then you will be financially secure." The Bible says, "Share with others in need, and what you sow you will reap." You cannot outgive God. Sharing with those in need is more than charity; it is smart finances and just good common sense.

Proverbs 19:17 reminds us, "He who is kind to the poor lends to *the Lord,* and he [God] will reward him for what he has done" (italics added). Never forget that God's investment program offers by far the best interest rates. The Bible has more promises in relation to money than almost any other topic. More than heaven and hell? Yes! More than love? Yes! More than faith? Yes! Why? Because it's so important and so difficult.

If my finances are not under God's control, then guess what? Not much of my life is under God's control.

You can tell a lot about people's walk with the Lord (what their priorities are) by looking at their schedules and their checkbook stubs. Generosity is a matter of faith. Proverbs 3:9–10 says, "Honor the Lord with your wealth, with the firstfruits of all your crops; then your barns will be filled to overflowing, and your vats will brim over with new wine." Why? I should be so thankful for what God has done in my life in the past that my heart overflows from an attitude of gratitude to Him in the present.

If you are struggling in this area, you might want to pray a prayer like this:

God, I realize that if You hadn't given me my health, I wouldn't have been able to make this money in the first place, and I realize that it all belongs to You anyway. Therefore, I want to give 10 percent back to You in gratitude.

When I get my paycheck and I sit down to write checks, I first write out my check for 10 percent. It is an act of faith and a continued pledge from a heart that is filled with faith and gratitude.

OUR RESPONSE

Life is a test, or a kind of boot camp. How we live these sixty, seventy, or eighty years determines how we will spend millions of years (Luke 16:19–31). If we do well on earth, we will be rewarded in heaven.

So, the big question I must seek an answer for is this: How do I do this? How do I learn this aspect of God's Top Ten List? Here are a few suggestions.

1. *Make restitution when necessary and possible.*

In Luke 19:8 we find the story of Zacchaeus, who needed to do just that. "Zacchaeus stood up and said to the Lord, 'Look, Lord! Here and now I give half of my possessions to the poor, and if I have cheated anybody out of anything, I will pay back four times the amount.'"

Zacchaeus was a tax collector. He didn't get paid except what he skimmed off the top. After just one meal with Jesus he was a new man. Exodus 22:1 says, "If a man steals an ox or a sheep and slaughters it and sells it, he must pay back five head of cattle for the ox and four sheep for the sheep." And Leviticus 6:4–5 says that lost property the guilty party found or what was stolen or taken by extortion or entrusted to him, "he must make restitution in full [and] add a fifth of the value to it." Zacchaeus had a legal obligation only to pay back the money he owed plus a fifth added to it, but he gave the requirement for someone who had stolen a sheep: quadruple repayment! After this Jesus said that salvation had come to his house.

Who do you owe that you haven't repaid? Have you borrowed things and not returned them? Have you ripped someone off? If you don't remember, ask God to help you. He remembers, and He wants to help you to

make restitution. Go out of your way to do it, and people will be impressed with both you and your God.

2. *Give others their due.*

Proverbs 21:3 says, "To do what is right and just is
more acceptable to the Lord than sacrifice." If you read
the Old Testament, you see that many of the instructions
had to do with the sacrifices. But here God makes it
clear what's more important. After all, though the sacrifices warranted many chapters, they still didn't make
God's Top Ten! Make fair deals. Don't rip others off or
take advantage of them. Do what is right.

3. *Give God His due.*

Use 10 percent as a guideline. Aim for it, and if
you're able, surpass it. Start slowly and work your way
there. It took Nancy and me a couple of years to get to
the full 10 percent. Now we're looking at 15 percent
someday. Why strive for more? Malachi 3:10 says,
"'Bring the whole tithe into the storehouse, that there
may be food in my house. Test me in this,' says the Lord
Almighty, 'and see if I will not throw open the floodgates
of heaven and pour out so much blessing that you will
not have room enough for it.'" Why not give it a try?
You've got nothing to lose and lots to gain!

4. *Make a living patiently and honestly.*

Again the wisdom of Solomon comes through.
Proverbs 13:11 says, "Dishonest money dwindles away,
but he who gathers money little by little makes it grow."
Don't go for the get-rich-quick schemes. Don't be tempted by greed, laziness, or pride. Make a plan to increase
little by little—patiently and honestly. Ephesians 4:28
says, "He who has been stealing must steal no longer,

but must work, doing something useful with his own hands, that he may have something to share with those in need." The key is not to acquire all we can; it's all a matter of management. Paul wrote in 1 Corinthians 4:1, "So then, men ought to regard us as servants of Christ and as those entrusted with the secret things of God."

I have spent many hours on airplanes traveling to and from speaking engagements. At one time the men and women who seated us and served us were called stewards and stewardesses, but now we call them flight attendants. I prefer the previous title because it reflects exactly what they have been called to do. They have been given the responsibility of care for the people and the aircraft to which they are assigned. They own neither, but have the trust of the company to get the goods from one place to another. The real authority belongs to the company, and these employees simply get to dispense it to the people.

We, likewise, are stewards. God has given us the stewardship of our time, our energies, our families, and our possessions. They are His—lock, stock, and barrel. All He asks of us is to take care of them, or manage them wisely.

Notes

1. Michael Hodgin, "Valid or Sound Arguments," *Parables, etc.*, 17, no. 9 (November 1997): 4.
2. Steven A. Pickert, "Organized Gardening," as quoted in *Parables, etc.*, 17, no. 8 (October 1997): 7.
3. Wayne Hollaway, from the Associated Press, quoted in *Parables, etc.* 17, no. 9 (November 1997): 3.

chapter ten

Telling the Truth

"You shall not give false testimony against your neighbor."
—Exodus 20:16

In the movie *Liar! Liar!* Jim Carey stars as a lawyer who is prone to lie and has probably been trained to lie. He has made numerous promises to his son and continually lets him down. After he fails to keep a promise to attend his son's birthday party, his son is almost ready to blow out the candles on his birthday cake when he is reminded to make a wish. His wish? "Please make my dad tell the truth for a whole day." For the next twenty-four hours revolutionary change and panic come into his father's life as he finds he can no longer lie. Every word that comes out of his mouth is the absolute truth. He now insults his friends, where at one time he lied. He now violates the trust of major clients, where at one time he would lie. Carey's life is absolutely chaotic for twenty-four hours as he learns the value and power of truth.

In chapter 1 I said that we live in a world filled with "truth decay." Who knows what the truth is, and who in our society even cares?

R. C. Sproul says:

What is truth? In his later years Francis Schaeffer frequently spoke of "true truth." What a strange expression. The phrase "true truth" is such an obvious redundancy we wonder why any one would be tempted to speak in this manner. It is like speaking of a circular circle or a squarish square or a beautiful beauty. Francis Schaeffer didn't stutter. He had a powerful reason to speak of true truth, and he used this terminology to distinguish what he was talking about from other popular notions of truth in our culture.[1]

I listen to the news on television and can't help but wonder if I'm getting the straight scoop. I hear so much double-talk: "I didn't steal; I borrowed." "I wasn't sleeping; I was resting my eyes." "They don't pay me what I'm worth; so I took." The result of all this doublespeak is a society in which we take everything that everybody says with a grain of salt—including those close to us. I have read secular studies on lie detectors and truth-telling where the general conclusion is that people are basically liars.

I believe Francis Schaeffer was right in saying, "We must not forget that the world is on fire. We are not only losing the church, but our entire culture as well. We live in a post-Christian world which is under the judgment of God."[2] Nowhere is this seen more than in telling the truth.

Yes, people lie, and their lies hurt others. But in contrast, God gives His people this ninth timeless principle, Exodus 20:16: "You shall not give false testimony against your neighbor." This principle is directly related to a nation's judicial system. The whole system hangs on the honesty of the people involved in the process. If one false witness is introduced into the system, someone who is willing to bend the truth, present only part of the truth, or even completely fabricate a story to harm another person, the result is injustice. Someone is falsely accused. Lives are ruined. Families are shamed.

Liar! Liar! is built on a pie-in-the-sky concept, but it doesn't work. We need a compelling reason to tell the truth. We need an inner compulsion to not lie despite the consequences. How about . . . God says so! You see, when God gave this ninth commandment to us, His command emphasized two things.

First, it emphasized *relationships*. Notice what God calls the person we are prone to lie about, with whom we are angry, or on whom we are seeking revenge. God doesn't call him an adversary or an enemy or even the opponent. He calls my adversary *neighbor,* reminding me of relationship. He reminds me that this person is a member of the human family, that he is a human being formed carefully by God, and that he matters. Proverbs 25:18 says: "Like a club or a sword or a sharp arrow is the man who gives false testimony against his neighbor." Proverbs 26:23 states: "Like a coating of glaze over earthenware are fervent lips with an evil heart." God always emphasizes relationships—the value of the other person who is harmed by my actions.

Second, it emphasized *integrity*. God also emphasizes the integrity and honesty required within the community of God. God's relation to Israel was based on His faithfulness, reliability, and trustworthiness. God's desire was for His people to reflect His faithfulness, not just in relationship to Him, but in relationship to each other (whether in legal, business, or personal transactions).

WHAT DID JESUS SAY?

Jesus emphasized a similar concept with His followers in Matthew 5:33–37.

"Again, you have heard that it was said to the people long ago, 'Do not break your oath, but keep the oaths you have made to the Lord.' But I tell you, Do not swear at all: either by heaven, for it is God's throne; or by the earth, for it is his footstool; or by Jerusalem, for it is the city of the Great King. And do not swear by your head, for you cannot make even one hair white or black. Simply let your 'Yes' be 'Yes,' and your 'No,' 'No'; anything beyond this comes from the evil one."

In Jesus' day, when people swore by God's name, it was considered binding, based in part on the third command: Don't treat the name of the Lord lightly! Over the years in that culture, certain loopholes developed. The degree to which an oath was judged to be binding was by examining how closely it related to God's name ("my good name," "my mother's grave," "heaven," "earth," "the temple"). Jesus attacked this entire mind-set. Your word—yes and no—must be as reliable as if swearing to God. After all, He is everywhere and part of every transaction in some way anyhow! The people of God must have absolute integrity and honesty.

TELL THE TRUTH
COMPLETELY AND CONSISTENTLY

The ramification of this command on our lives is twofold. First and foremost God calls us to tell the truth *completely* and *consistently*. A half truth is a whole lie. How does a person tell the truth incompletely and inconsistently? One way is simply *by not saying all we mean*. We know we're thinking or feeling something we're not disclosing. Or we say something in a way that we hope the listeners will not see past to see the truth. For example, have you ever finished off the milk and had your spouse say, "Did you take the last of the milk?"

You respond straight-faced with "Honey, would I do that?" So your spouse doesn't pursue it, thinking, *Of course he (she) would not. One of the children must have emptied the carton.* And the lie is bought.

It's as though we have no conscience, or at least are afraid to live by it. John MacArthur writes, "The conscience is generally seen by the modern world as a defect that robs people of their self-esteem. Far from being a defect or disorder, however, our ability to sense our own guilt is a tremendous gift from God."[3]

The second way not to tell the truth completely is by *not meaning all we say.* This is where the whole area of doublespeak plays a role. We flatter; we make false promises and commitments. What's the effect of all this? Destruction. Proverbs 11:3 declares, "The integrity of the upright guides them, but the unfaithful are destroyed by their duplicity."

Honesty in a relationship is a lot like the sun to plants. Relationships thrive on honesty and wither when it is withheld. So as we let the warmth of honesty shine on a relationship, it grows and it thrives. But when the darkness of a lie casts a shadow on a relationship, the relationship starts to wither, just as a sun-loving plant when put into the shade.

TELL THE TRUTH
COMPASSIONATELY AND CAREFULLY

The second ramification of this commandment is to tell the truth compassionately and carefully. Ephesians 4:15 speaks to this issue of truth as Paul wrote, "Instead, speaking the truth in love, we will in all things grow up into him who is the Head, that is, Christ." We grow into Christian maturity in a context where truth is lived out in love. The concept of truth here refers directly to

Christian truth—the truth of the good news regarding Jesus Christ. Unadulterated truth is sometimes hard to swallow (even demeaning and hurtful) when not given in love. So Christian truth always holds in tension the two dynamics of truth and love.

Christ Himself ultimately embodied the two. John 1:14 says, "The Word became flesh and made his dwelling among us. We have seen his glory, the glory of the One and Only, who came from the Father, full of grace and truth." We, too, seeking to be *completely* honest, must become *compassionately* honest. If we don't learn this, the consequences are extremely painful. Proverbs 12:18 talks to this area of how our words can invoke pain or blessing: "Reckless words pierce like a sword, but the tongue of the wise brings healing."

I find it interesting how Proverbs describes the person who speaks recklessly as worse than a fool. Proverbs 29:20: "Do you see a man who speaks in haste? There is more hope for a fool than for him." In contrast, the wise person weighs words, considers *how* to say things, and thus brings *healing*. Some people pride themselves in their bluntness. I see no scriptural support for truth without love. There are people who can give a compliment, but you walk away feeling insulted. There are people who can give criticism, yet you walk away feeling enriched. Because relationships are as important as truth, speaking the truth compassionately is just as important as speaking it completely.

THE LIES WE TELL

All this talk about truth has probably left you feeling pretty guilty. Let's look at the reality. Mark Twain is credited with saying, "There are two kinds of lies: Bold face lies and statistics." Doing extensive research for speaking and writing has reminded me of this. However, I want to broaden my categories a little and list what I believe are five distinct categories of lies.

1. *The cruel lie*

These include lies that are intentionally malicious and destructive. A prime example of this kind of lie is often seen in the political arena. Politicians can be ruthless as they slander one another, seeking to damage their opponents' reputations. The motive for this kind of lie is often resentment. Politicians who attack opponents are trying to replace or remove the adversaries' input and livelihood. Therefore, with a resentful motive, they do whatever it takes to maintain their level of influence or importance.

2. *The cowardly lie*

This lie is merely an attempt to escape the consequences and protect yourself. Your boss walks up to you at work and asks, "So, how's that report coming along?" You are nowhere near finishing the report and are afraid to admit your miscalculation of time, so you say, "I'm finishing that report right now." A creditor calls about a payment. You are in a financial pinch and have "robbed Peter to pay Paul." Yet you tell the creditor, "The check's in the mail." What's the motive for such cowardly lies? Fear! You are afraid your boss will discover your incompetence. You're afraid to admit your financial planning inadequacies. You are afraid, so you lie.

3. *The conceited lie*

This is where we inflate ourselves so we can impress others. Some might call this lie bragging. It's time to change jobs and the market has become very competitive in your field, so you pad your résumé. The motive for the conceited lie is insecurity. We're afraid that people will learn the truth about us and not like us nor not hire us. So we lie. An underlying part of this lie is our lack of trust in God that He will provide. We feel we have to take things into our own hands if we are to get what we are seeking.

4. *The calculated lie*

We manipulate others to get our way. This manipulation is what I sometimes feel when I'm out buying a car. The salesman is so slick, so precise with the ruse of having to "ask" the manager if he can make a deal. The same precision is applied when the manager comes into the room like a tag-team partner and continues to push for the sale. The motive for this lie is greed. I lie because I want to get my way. I'm selfish and so push to eat at a certain restaurant by calculating a lie about the food at the other restaurant.

5. *The convenient lie*

This lie happens when it's going to take effort, time, or energy to tell the truth. I can remember being invited to a party and saying I planned to attend when I had no intention of ever going near the party. Why didn't I just say, "You know, I am just too busy. Thanks for the invitation, but I'm going to have to pass"? I'll tell you why. The motive for this lie is laziness. It would either take some emotional energy to explain why I wouldn't be there or some physical effort on my part to follow through on my commitment.

A MATTER OF THE HEART

In Jewish thinking the site of real understanding was the heart. Of course, in our culture the heart is often associated with emotions. "I love you with all my heart." But to the original readers of Scripture, the heart represented life experience and the base of knowledge. With this in mind, we begin to understand more clearly passages like Matthew 12:34: "You brood of vipers, how can you who are evil say anything good? For out of the overflow of the heart the mouth speaks."

Matthew 5:19 adds this insight: "Anyone who breaks one of the least of these commandments and teaches others to do the same will be called least in the kingdom of heaven, but whoever practices and teaches these commands will be called great in the kingdom of heaven." It appears that issues like resentment, greed, fear, laziness, and insecurity are all matters of the heart. To become people of honesty and integrity requires more than just feeling good about honesty and truth. The solution? A new heart. Jesus specializes in heart transplants. When you accept Christ into your life, you aren't just "turning over a new leaf," you are starting a whole new life. Second Corinthians 5:17 says, "Therefore, if anyone is in Christ, he is a new creation; the old has gone, the new has come!"

The best thing to do if you are struggling with this area of honesty is to admit it to the Lord and ask the Holy Spirit to help you. Your prayer might be something like this:

Lord, You know I really struggle in the area of being 100 percent honest 100 percent of the time. I want to be, and I know You want me to be. But I am weak and have not been able to be successful in my own strength. So if I am ever to be a truthful person, You will need to give me Your strength to resist the temptation to lie. Holy Spirit, I need You to make me aware of when I am about to shade the truth, and then give me the right words to say and the courage to say them.

By the way, this prayer is good to use for any weakness you have.

TELLING THE WHOLE TRUTH

God never intended for us to gain knowledge without changing our hearts and our actions. Scripture is God's textbook for us to change. This aspect of truthtelling is a massive problem in our world today. How can we be a part of the answer to this question of "truth decay"? What would God have us do if we desire to follow this ninth principle on His Top Ten List? Here are some ideas.

Confess Your Dishonesty to God and Others

I have learned in my walk with God to keep short accounts with Him and others. Each of us has a life experience that includes our upbringing, accumulated knowledge, and memories of the good and bad times, which tend to create a filter through which we judge things. Let's say you accumulate more knowledge. You read about becoming a better parent. You attend a seminar on becoming a better boss. You discuss the life experience with your mate at a marital retreat where you are challenged to greater levels of commitment and communication. Then a gap forms. This gap often manifests itself as guilt:

Greater Knowledge

GUILT

Life Experience

How do you close this gap? First John 1:8–9 says, "If we claim to be without sin, we deceive ourselves and the truth is not in us. If we confess our sins, he is faithful and just and will forgive us our sins and purify us from all unrighteousness." When we learn to confess our sins, instead of hiding them, we will naturally deal with the guilt we carry around as excess baggage and close the gap and reduce the stress of guilt:

Greater Knowledge

Life Experience

Too often we gather knowledge and forget that a part of the process of healing in our lives is confession. James 5:16 says, "Therefore confess your sins to each other and pray for each other so that you may be healed. The prayer of a righteous man is powerful and effective." There's nothing quite like stepping into the light in order to break the power of something. I do a lot of counseling in my church and have heard people confess some horrendous things. But it's when someone says to me, "Glen, I have never admitted this to anyone before," that I know a breakthrough is about to occur. The first step of any recovery program is to admit you have a problem. If our Lord said, "The truth will set you free," then it stands to reason that the truth is *always* freeing.

Commit to Complete, Compassionate Honesty

Before I became a Christian in high school, I was very dishonest. Cheating on tests was the norm because I was competing for scholarship positioning. Lying to teachers and coaches was the easy way to advance my goals. But after I became a Christian, I made a commitment to ruthless honesty.

This is the difference when you become a person of integrity. This means taking the step in prayer that was

covered above in "A Matter of the Heart." Then you need
each evening (or the next morning at the latest), to evaluate your day, asking the Holy Spirit to show you any
way in which you have not been completely truthful.
You will want to ask Him to show you what you should
have said. As part of being "squeaky clean" in this area,
you will need to go to the person involved and tell him
the truth. *Ouch!* I know from experience that hurts, but
if you really are sincere with the Lord, you will commit
yourself to this level of honesty.

It is important, as you see you have been less than
honest, not to buy the lie from the Enemy that you are
always going to be a liar and can never be strong enough
to break this habit. That is not true. Philippians 4:13
promises that you can do all things through the strength
the Lord gives you. So when you sin, confess it, thank
the Lord for His forgiveness, and then thank Him that
He is in the process of helping you become a truthful
person. In this way you are expressing your faith in the
ongoing work He is doing in your life.

Surround Yourself with God's Truth

Living in the world today you are surrounded by lies.
"When a relationship is difficult, bail! You deserve better!" *God's perspective:* Relationships are eternal. Mend
and preserve them. Love in bed involves a public, lasting
commitment, and when that is present it is incredibly
rewarding.

Another lie: "Do what feels good. Don't let anyone
tell you what to do." *God's perspective:* There are timeless, eternal principles that govern lives. When you go
against them, you hurt yourself and others.

A third lie: "Truth is obsolete. Relative. You can't be
sure of truth." *Jesus said,* "You will know the truth, and

the truth will set you free" (John 8:32). How? Our Lord also said, "I am the way and the truth and the life" (John 14:6).

One last lie: "You don't matter," or "You only matter for what you do or how you look." *God's perspective:* "You matter to Me because I love you." His love for us originates from who He is. It is not dependent on how famous or talented we are, or what we do, or how we look. His love, not our loveliness, causes Him to love us.

Let's be practical here. If surrounding yourself with the truth of the Bible is essential to personal growth and holiness, we need to know ways of doing just that. Here are three.

1. *Spend time in God's Word.*

When you do this, you are learning what God's standards are and you are able to correct any wrong or fuzzy thinking that has allowed you to rationalize your lying.

Proverbs 6:16–19 zeros in on God's feelings. "There are six things the Lord hates, seven that are detestable to him: haughty eyes, a lying tongue, hands that shed innocent blood, a heart that devises wicked schemes, feet that are quick to rush into evil, a false witness who pours out lies and a man who stirs up dissension among brothers." Notice that two of the seven have to do with not saying the truth—a lying tongue and a false witness. When you see how God hates lying, putting it twice on a list that does not even include adultery, you will recognize that what we in today's society tend to excuse, He holds as a grievous sin. Pretty heavy! So you need the Word to help you know how to avoid lies and lay the foundation of truthfulness at the core of your being.

Do you really grasp how important the Bible is to our lives? Carl F. Henry once wrote, "The fate of the

Bible is the fate of Christianity and even of civilization itself. If the world neglects or evangelicals forsake this Book, the end result is society's inevitable theological, spiritual, and moral suicide."[4] Listen, if the Bible is this important—and it is—doesn't it make sense to spend a little more time studying it?

2. *Spend time with truthful people.*

God addressed this issue directly in 1 Corinthians 15:33–34: "Do not be misled: 'Bad company corrupts good character.' Come back to your senses as you ought." This is the equivalent of the world's parable of the bad apple in the barrel of good apples that can spoil all of them. Folks, it's a fact of life. If you hang out with those who do not tell the truth, it will affect your thought process, and you will have a greater tendency to compromise because of their influence. Ask God to show you the people He wants you to associate with. You can also ask Him to remove you from the presence of those who are dishonest and may have been influencing you. Another thing you can do is to ask Him to block their input into your thought processes if they are people you work with or otherwise cannot avoid.

3. *Spend time thinking about the truth.*

Probably one of the best pieces of advice I can give you in this area is to memorize some Bible passages. This gives the Holy Spirit material to focus your mind on, something to remind you about when you are about to be less than truthful.

4. *Entrust yourself to God's care.*

Many people are paralyzed as they struggle with fear, insecurity, and greed. They say, "God, help me to be more interested in character than reputation." Being completely and compassionately honest won't come naturally. It will cost something! But as we "entrust ourselves to God's care," we choose to believe Him, to rely on Him to watch over us. We say, "God will take care of me." When was the last time you said that? Say it right now: "God will take care of me!" For some, this is much harder to say than they think. Though being honest may cause me to lose a sale or business deal, *God will take care of me.* Though being honest may mean temporary strains on relationships, maybe even an argument with my spouse or a friend, *God will take care of me.* Though being honest may mean temporary humility or loss of face as I own up to things, *God will take care of me.* Though being honest may result in the loss of a promotion, possibly even loss of my job, *God will take care of me.* Though being honest may take more effort, time, and energy in my life, *God will take care of me.*

CONCLUSION

A little girl had a bad habit. She was always lying. When she was given a St. Bernard dog for her birthday, she went out and told all the neighbors that she had been given a lion. The mother took her aside and said, "I told you not to lie. You go upstairs and tell God you are sorry. Promise God you will not lie again." The little girl went upstairs, said her prayers, then came down again. Her mother asked, "Did you tell God you are sorry?" The little girl replied, "Yes, I did. And God said sometimes He finds it hard to tell my dog from a lion too."[5]

You won't get much plainer than this. Proverbs 12:22 says, "The Lord detests lying lips, but he delights in men who are truthful." Friends, you can be a person God delights in no matter what is true of you now. Simply ask

Him for His help. Recognize that with men it is impossible, but with God nothing is impossible. Ask Him to make it your heart's desire to be truthful all the time and to make your emotions at the point of weakness fall into line with His desires.

Draw on the Holy Spirit's power to do this, and you can and will see Him make the necessary changes in your life. Believe me, this will not only please Him, but it will please those around you and will bring delight and peace to your own heart as you overcome something that has been a source of guilt throughout your life. To really feel clean in this area, to know you are pleasing the Lord and others, is well worth the effort it will take to be a truthful person.

Notes

1. R. C. Sproul, *The Character of God* (Ann Arbor, Mich.: Vine, 1995), 136.
2. Francis Schaeffer, *The Great Evangelical Disaster* (Westchester, Ill.: Crossway, 1984), 90.
3. John F. MacArthur, Jr., *The Vanishing Conscience* (Dallas: Word, 1994), 36.
4. Carl F. Henry, *The Christian Mindset in a Secular Society* (Portland: Multnomah, 1984), 34.
5. Illustration from *Sunday Sermons Treasury of Illustrations,* 2:320, as quoted in *The Pastor's Story File,* July 1985 (P.O. Box 8, 311 Elizabeth Ave., Suite B, Platteville, CO 80651-0008).

loving **GOD**
and being content

"Therefore I tell you, do not worry about your life, what you will eat or drink; or about your body, what you will wear. Is not life more important than food, and the body more important than clothes? Look at the birds of the air; they do not sow or reap or store away in barns, and yet your heavenly Father feeds them. Are you not much more valuable than they? Who of you by worrying can add a single hour to his life?

"And why do you worry about clothes? See how the lilies of the field grow. They do not labor or spin. Yet I tell you that not even Solomon in all his splendor was dressed like one of these. If that is how God clothes the grass of the field, which is here today and tomorrow is thrown into the fire, will he not much more clothe you, O you of little faith? So do not worry saying, 'What shall we eat?' or 'What shall we drink?' or 'What shall we wear?' For the pagans run after all these things, and your heavenly Father knows that you need them. But seek first his kingdom and his righteousness, and all these things will be given to you as well."

—Matthew 6:25–33

chapter eleven

Content or Discontent?

"You shall not covet your neighbor's house. You shall not covet your neighbor's wife, or his manservant or maidservant, his ox or donkey, or anything that belongs to your neighbor."

—Exodus 20:17

Did you know that the Lord Jesus Christ spoke more about a person's relationship to possessions than He spoke about baptism, His Second Coming, judgment, Holy Communion, and the Word of God all put together? It was an important point of teaching two thousand years ago, and it's equally important today.

Americans spend twice as much on alcohol as on charitable giving and nearly five times as much on recreation. My question is, Why? Because America doesn't understand what God's view is concerning our possessions. We are so bent on keeping up with our neighbors and collecting as much as our relatives that we have climbed into the trap of discontentment and now have become a covetous nation.

Today the word we would use to describe the word

covet is the word *materialism,* simply wanting to obtain things. Television commercials, billboards, and magazines bombard us with advertising about getting more. I remember my initiation into this media frenzy. Watching the television as a child I heard, "If it isn't a Duncan, it isn't a yo-yo." One of my earliest birthdays found my parents trying to sneak into my life a completely counterfeit yo-yo. I opened the package, looked for the correct insignia, and then declared, "This ain't no yo-yo; it's not a Duncan." The advertisers had been successful in generating discontentment within me.

It's no secret that America has become extremely materialistic. Milton Bradley's new board game, "Mall Madness," demonstrates just how far this materialism has developed. The goal of the game is to be the first person to lose all your money. Only when you have emptied all your pockets and have released every cent to your name can you jump into the "winner's circle" and be declared broke!

Ask the average teenaged girl what she loves to do for fun—shop. Sit down and chat with some people who live a fast-paced lifestyle and ask them what they love to do to release stress—shop. Frequently, this materialism is powered by comparison with others. After all, the grass is always greener on the other side. Just look at the smiling people in the ads, the next-door neighbor who has it together, and the peace of mind apparently achieved by ownership. "In our never-satisfied culture, materialism is not only a way of life, it is part of the American Dream. Turn on your television, read a magazine, or talk with friends over dinner and you will see that life's greatest struggles can and will be answered by attaining and achieving. After all, 'You deserve a break today' because 'You're worth it.'"[1]

Our environment thrives on the "If only" syndrome. "If only I had a bigger paycheck, then I'd be happy." "If only we owned a nicer home." "If only I had that car." If we live in the correct place, wear the right clothes, and enjoy vacations at the choicest spots, we've arrived.

Too many people struggle with "destination disease," desperately hoping that life and family will be better when they arrive. Most reach midlife crying out, "Stop the world—I want to get off," or "Get me out of this rat race!" But they are afraid of "stopping their world," fearful that it will suddenly stop and throw them into a worse situation. "So they stay in their rat race world, and suffer, usually not so silently, getting more and more frustrated as their life races out of control."[2] We find working moms jealous of a stay-at-home friend's lifestyle, whereas the stay-at-home mom envies her friend's vocational accomplishments. Is anyone ever happy with the life God has given him?

The grass-is-greener syndrome is nothing new. From the very beginning, people have been comparing, measuring their blessings from God against someone else's blessings. So, God concludes His Top Ten List with this command: "You shall not covet your neighbor's house. You shall not covet your neighbor's wife, or his manservant or maidservant, his ox or donkey, or anything that belongs to your neighbor"(Exodus 20:17).

In one sentence, God provides a focus on the problem and an answer to the stress of competition we all feel. The idea of coveting is simply that uncontrolled desire to acquire what other people have. This can be the *material*—a beautiful home, expensive cars, jewelry, financial success. It can be *family*—an attractive spouse, intelligent children, famous relatives. It can be *personal* —good looks, an outgoing personality, intellectual gifts, a degree from an Ivy League school. It can be the immaterial—prestige and authority, a joyful spirit, a sense of peace.

In choosing to conclude with this command, God gives it a position of emphasis. The apostle Paul said, "Is the law sin? Certainly not! Indeed I would not have known what sin was except through the law. For I would not have known what coveting really was if the law had not said, 'Do not covet'" (Romans 7:7). All of the sins mentioned in the other nine commandments in some way relate to covetousness. And even if we could avoid breaking the other nine sins, if we covet, we have broken the whole law. Satan saw the glory of God and wanted it for himself. Judas Iscariat saw financial gain in betraying Christ. Ananias and Sapphira thought they could gain social approval in the church without having to hurt themselves financially. David sought Uriah's spouse for himself and ended up committing adultery and arranging for a murder.

Unlike the rest of the commands, coveting can't be seen from outside. It is something going on inside, at the heart of my passions and desires. God says that what's going on in your private world is as crucial as what's going on in your public world. Coveting may seem private, but it is a sin against other people and ingratitude to God.

My wife, Nancy, and I lived in a tiny, six-hundred-square-foot apartment when we were first married. Living in a poor part of town, but close to our university, our only aspiration was to break into the middle class, which we defined as having a two-bedroom apartment. Actually buying a home was beyond our wildest dreams. About four years later, we purchased our first home, a modest two-bedroom home in desperate need of some minor care like paint, repairs, and lots of yard work. But living in that home was a touch of heaven. We could make do with two or three hours of yard work each week and periodic sanding of the hardwood floors.

Or could we? After two-and-a-half years, we discovered we were no longer satisfied. The newness of home ownership had worn off. We found ourselves on the prowl, searching for a larger, newer, three-bedroom home.

Three homes later we are truly content, or are we? In the midst of our never-enough world, there is always plenty more to want, and I've made a startling realization—always wanting is symptomatic of life in the Rat Race.[3]

WHAT'S THE BIG DEAL ABOUT COVETING?

Max Anders, in the introduction to his book *The Good Life*, says:

> Wealth, purpose, love and power. If we have those, we say, we have it all. Unfortunately, instead of the "real thing," we too often settle for a substitute. We are content with cheap—and dangerous—imitations. Instead of wealth, we grab money. Instead of purpose, we settle for ambition. Instead of love, we grab sex. Instead of power, we take clout. No matter how appealing, of course, the substitute never really satisfies.[4]

Isn't that the truth? But nonetheless we covet another person's new car, nice suit, or new home, just hoping the desire will then fade. Let's look at what's wrong with coveting.

A Lack of Appreciation for God's Provision

I suspect that when we respond to our abundance with dissatisfaction and an insatiable desire to acquire more, God must see it as an incredible affront to His generosity and an unbelievable act of ingratitude. It reminds me of the five-year-old who sits near the Christmas tree, hardly visible among all the wrapping paper he has tossed around. As he looks at the hoard of gifts he's received, he looks crestfallen and starts to cry. Why? Because he did not get the red Power Ranger he wanted, even though every other desire was fulfilled.

A Lack of Faith in God's Goodness

In the battle we wage with the Enemy of our souls, faith plays a key part. Satan is constantly trying to get us to mistrust God, to think that He is not a good God or does not want the best for us or has a hidden agenda He will spring on us if we trust Him. So, essentially, our ability to appreciate what God has given us and refuse comparison with what others have is an issue of *faith*. Do we trust God that if we are lacking something, then there is a good reason for it? Or do we instead listen to the doubts, the accusations against Him that are whispered in our ears?

Hebrews 13:5–6 exhorts us, "Keep your lives free from the love of money and be content with what you have, because God has said, 'Never will I leave you; never will I forsake you.' So we say with confidence, 'The Lord is my helper; I will not be afraid. What can man do to me?'" Do you believe these verses? Is God truly honest with us when He makes these promises? It boils down to this: We need to ask ourselves some searching questions.

- Will I believe God? Will I trust His goodness, acceptance, and favor?
- Do I trust Him to take care of me?
- Do I need to fend for myself instead?

A Lack of Compassion for My Neighbor

Coveting what my neighbor has—a better job, nicer home, cooler toys, more relaxing vacations—is destructive to our relationship. It allows walls to be built up between us, because I am dissatisfied and he is the perceived cause of it. But my neighbor is not just another Joe. He is someone I should be friends with. I should be glad when he succeeds and is able to get something nice. He is a fellow human being about whose well-being I should be concerned.

How do you react when you see someone with nicer stuff? Are you glad for the person, or do you give in to that green-eyed monster of envy? For many this is not just a saying. Envy has become monstrous in their lives as they have let it take over, dictate how they spend their money, and even tell them how happy and contented they can be at any given time. The stress, anxiety, and even bitterness and anger that can come from envy are destructive.

Although none of us would knowingly take a poisonous reptile to our bosom, spiritually many of us have embraced envy and allowed it to poison our hearts and souls. None of us would welcome and assist a thief in stealing our possessions, yet the one who allows envy to be present allows a thief, even a murderer, to be part of his life. And the results can only be disastrous.

You may be thinking, *What's the big deal about coveting?* It is a matter of the heart! When our hearts are right with God, they will be right with His creation. So if you are feeling covetous in any area, you need to ask yourself if you have

• a heart that is thankful,

- a heart full of faith, and
- a heart that cares about others.

Warning! What we are looking at is not just a minor thing. Our desire to acquire has destructive side effects. In 1 Timothy 6:9 we read, "People who want to get rich fall into temptation and a trap and into many foolish and harmful desires that plunge men into ruin and destruction." Covetousness destroys our relationship with God, skews our finances, impedes our relationships, and tears down our self-worth. So it is important to see if you recognize any of these elements in your life. If you do, take the necessary steps to correct your heart attitude.

EFFECTS OF OUR DESIRE FOR MORE

Our ingrown propensity to get more, achieve more, and have more affects us in a variety of ways.

Fatigue

In the push to get more, we take on more and more. How do we fund this monster of desire we've nurtured? By working longer and longer hours, of course; or maybe even getting a second job or having the wife of the family work when it really wouldn't be necessary for her to do that if our desires were brought into balance. This leads to fatigue. We get exhausted trying to earn the money to pay for all our spending. We get exhausted doing the shopping, even though we may first experience a temporary high. We get uptight and worn out trying to figure out how we're going to pay all our bills.

God knew what He was doing when He warned us of the dangers of coveting. He knew that coveting can easily rob our children of much of the love and nurture they need, as their parents spend longer and longer hours working so they can get things. We also set a miserable example for our children of how to handle money and of where our priorities are. Covetousness is nothing if not a lose-lose situation. No one wins; everyone loses. This is why Solomon warned us in Proverbs 23:4, "Do not wear yourself out to get rich; have the wisdom to show restraint."

Dissatisfaction

Covetousness is like fire—it can never be satisfied. It is like feeding a lot of meat to a lion and expecting it to become a vegetarian someday as you try to "satisfy" its need for meat. No, the more you feed your desire to "get more," the greater appetite you create for things. Have you ever found yourself with extra money in your pocket or checkbook and decided to indulge the urge to go to the store and see what you might buy, even though there is nothing in particular you need? Most of us have. Satisfying such desires can be very harmful to our mental health.

The more we give in to our desires, the more we will want to feed them, and in turn the more we are addicted to shopping. Even as I write these words, a large, nationwide department store chain features in a holiday ad a woman who has just heard of an eight-hour sale. She is so excited she is almost uncontrollable as she makes her plans. She starts by getting tennis shoes so she can run from department to department, and she joyously exclaims, "I'm going to be there all eight hours!" What a picture. And will she be satisfied when she comes home, staggering under her load of merchandise? Of course not. She will probably not even use some of the items, and others will soon be left in the closet or on the shelf, no longer holding the appeal they had on the sale day because they were not true necessities, but only greed.

Is it any wonder the richest man in the world, who could buy anything and everything his heart desired, warned us in Ecclesiastes 5:10, "Whoever loves money never has money enough; whoever loves wealth is never satisfied with his income. This too is meaningless." How true! It is said that when the multimillionaire J. P. Morgan was asked when a wealthy man has enough money to be happy, he replied, "When he has made the next million."

When asked how much money was enough, multimillionaire John D. Rockefeller responded candidly, "Just one dollar more." You know, folks, it is impossible for things to make us happy, because God did not create us to be fulfilled by them.

Three things satisfy the human soul: being safe and secure, giving and receiving love, and being a part of something greater than ourselves. But covetousness does not contribute to any of these three. Quite the contrary. It often destroys them. In coveting we sacrifice relationships for "stuff."

Debt

Our desire for more leads to a third negative: debt. The U.S. credit card debt is more than $206.7 billion. In fact, if you count home mortgages, the average American has $1,300 in debt for every $1,000 he makes. Large credit card balances, loans, bounced checks, and the like are symptoms of a heart that is not satisfied, that has desires the person has decided to fulfill even though fiscally it is a disaster to do so. In our modern society being in debt no longer holds the same stigma it did for our parents or grandparents. Those who came through the Depression, who lived in a wartime economy of rationing, learned to be frugal, to make every penny count.

I have a friend whose grandfather lived in Fresno, worked as an engineer during the Depression, and walked five miles one way to save the ten-cent bus ride. Most of us today will not even stoop down to pick up a dime. (But my friend does pick up those dimes and the pennies!)

Most of us think nothing of spending many dollars on frivolous things. That is, we don't think about it until we get so far into debt we cannot see over the stack of bills. Only then do we think of living more closely within our means. Talk about closing the barn door after the cows have gotten out! No wonder bankruptcies are at an all-time disastrous high. Even our government can't live within its means.

Debt is a killer. God knows that. This is why He addressed the issue in this tenth command. He didn't want us to worship things or to cripple our relationships by seeing others as competitors. He didn't want us to suffer the negatives that come with coveting material riches for ourselves.

Worry

We've looked at the stress that comes from how to pay the bills, but there is another kind of stress that covetousness causes, and that is our fourth element: worry. Ecclesiastes 5:12 puts it this way: "The sleep of a laborer is sweet, whether he eats little or much, but the abundance of a rich man permits him no sleep."

Our *thoughts* are, "Now that I have it, how can I protect it, invest it, diversify it, shelter it from taxes, and *keep* it?" Is it worth it all? You tell me! It has been my observation that insomnia does not increase one's income. But insomnia will increase with income.

Conflict

This brings us to the next step in the destructive effect of covetousness: conflict. Meeting normal financial needs can be a significant source of tension in relationships, especially in marriage. Add to this the conflict of unnecessary buying to fulfill artificially created "needs," and you have a powder keg. James puts it this way in James 4:1–2: "What causes fights and quarrels among you? Don't they come from your desires that battle within you? You want something but don't get it. You kill and covet, but you cannot have what you want. You quarrel and fight. You do not have, because you do not ask God."

It is sobering to realize that the number one cause of divorce is financial tension. Unfortunately, the tension doesn't decrease as income increases. In fact, statistics show that 90 percent of California lottery married winners end up getting divorced after winning.

Clinical psychologist David Stoop says that strained relationships are often a by-product of the grass-is-greener syndrome. Comparers sometimes distance themselves from those around them because they feel inadequate, jealous, or frustrated by those with whom they're competing.

Men, we play a significant role in this. We are always wanting to prove our manhood, our ability to be good providers by buying, buying, buying, especially if those we know are getting things we desire.

How true is Proverbs 15:27, "A greedy man brings trouble to his family."

How can we break the cycle of the grass-is-greener syndrome?

THREE WAYS TO BE
SATISFIED WITH WHAT YOU HAVE

The Bible is clear. We are to be satisfied with what we have. But our sinful human nature fights us at every step, wanting more and more, always comparing, always competing, always suspicious that we are not as blessed as our neighbor, do not have as many toys as the next person, or have not received the honors we deserve. So how do we break this hold that sin has on us? Here are three practical steps that will help you take control of your life in this area by bringing every thought under the control of Jesus (2 Corinthians 10:2–5) and reprogramming your mind to look at things from God's perspective.

Refuse to Compare Yourself to Others

At the root of comparison is a feeling of inadequacy, smallness, weakness, and insecurity. There is also an element of pride. All of this is the result of sin. We are self-centered and have an unrealistic view of others. We can too easily feel threatened by others or want to compete with them in order to prove to ourselves and to the world that we are worthwhile and the better person—that we are the winner! Many people fixate on their weaknesses and their neighbors' strengths rather than seeing themselves as unique persons of great value whom God has made.

The result: an inaccurate standard of comparison, which leads to a false view of self, circumstances, and God. Note: This can be unbalanced at either extreme of the spectrum: "I'm not as good as other people" or "I'm better than anyone I know."

Paul understood this problem. That's why he says in 2 Corinthians 10:12, "We do not dare to classify or compare ourselves with some who commend themselves. When they measure themselves by themselves and compare themselves with themselves, *they are not wise*" (italics added).

Do you struggle with comparing yourself to others? If so, there is hope in *Three Steps Out of the Comparison Trap,* by Randy Carlson. Here are his three steps, with some thoughts of my own.

1. *Recognize your comparing thought patterns.*

By identifying when and why you compare, you take one step closer to contentment. Ask the Lord to help you break this pattern. Choose to give up your right to compare.

2. *Prepare a comparison inventory.*

Write down the names of people you compare yourself with, and ask what it is about each person that points out your own inadequacies and self-pride. Then ask the Lord to give you His perspective, the truth about these areas. Next, choose to look at them His way from then on.

3. *Tell yourself the truth.*

After you've made your list, remind yourself that each person on it is inadequate, but you're all loved and accepted by God anyway. Believe that He does not want you competing with others but, rather, living contentedly together.

Enjoy What God Has Given You

One of our major problems today is that we simply do not enjoy the things God has provided and thus find ourselves searching and grasping for more. Could it be that if we learned to enjoy where we are in life right now, and enjoyed what God has provided right now, that this principle on God's Top Ten List would no longer be an issue in our lives? Ecclesiastes 5:19 says, "Moreover, when God gives any man wealth and possessions, and enables him to enjoy them, to accept his lot and be happy in his work—this is a gift of God."

Appreciate what you have; be grateful. Cultivate thankfulness as a discipline. Stop and think about how sad you'd be if you lost everything you have. Then think about how happy you'd be if you got it all back again. Make a list of everything you have, and thank God for it. Be sure to list nonmaterial wealth. One family I know of has a "Thank You Book," complete with pictures, devoted to recording answers to prayer and other blessings.

Men have a particularly difficult time enjoying the process and the moment. We're geared to be "conquerors," overcoming the next challenge, the next mountain. We need to slow down and "smell the coffee." For me, that means having to consciously say "Thank You" periodically to the Lord for the things He has provided, especially the things I longed for that He supplied. Otherwise, I lose my thankfulness too easily and take for granted that I now have this necessity or desire of my heart.

Enjoy!

Here are some things you need to enjoy . . . *right now!*

1. *Your mate*

Some are beginning to say that parents should stick together for kids. I'm saying something more . . . *enjoy him or her!* You loved and enjoyed the person while you were dating, so now you should be able to enjoy him or her even more.

Paul challenges men to love their wives just like Christ loves the church. This is an all-encompassing, tenderhearted love that is unconditional. If you are having a hard time loving your mate that way because of problems and struggles the two of you have had, admit it, and ask Him to help you see and love your mate the way He sees and loves him or her.

Part of enjoying your wife or husband will spill over to your children. One writer said: "The first step in being a great father is to love your wife."

Let your kids see your affection for your mate. Model to them what it means for a man to love a woman, and vice versa, in a positive, healthy way. Compliment your mate in front of the kids.

Another way to show appreciation is to bring home a special gift and have your mate open it during dinner. If she loves flowers, bring her a bouquet once in a while or put a fresh flower on her pillow. If he enjoys a good book, surprise him.

Here are some of the things your positive actions toward their other parent do for your kids:

- You model healthy relationships—commitment, teamwork, conflict resolution.
- Your communication of affection is good.
- You increase feelings of safety and security.

They need to see you love and respect your spouse. Particularly if you are a man, this is good for your wife too. A wife is easily taken for granted because she does so much for her family day in and day out. It gets to the point that members just expect her to do all her work without really noting how much it is or how she puts special effort into things like a meal, a party, or the way the home looks.

One other thing I would want to say to you men reading this: When you give her a gift, don't make it something for the kitchen or that helps with household chores. Wives get slighted this way too much.

2. *Your kids*

Create a sense of playfulness. Children need to feel free to touch others and be touched in appropriate ways. Playfulness helps teach them this. One of the things that a dad brings to the parenting relationship is the enjoyment of playing, such as wrestling, tickling, playing hide-and-seek, even teasing that is nondestructive.

Ken Canfield, director of the National Center for Fathering, boiled down the job description of a dad to five things. Here are two.

1. Make a conscious effort to involve yourself in your kids' activities. Regular physical involvement will bring about playful interaction—and both are important.
2. Think of the funniest thing that happened to you as a kid, and make sure your children hear it so much that they have it memorized.

3. *Your things*

Read Ecclesiastes 5:19 again. Does it surprise you that God wants you to enjoy things? It surprised me. Did you know that in the Old Testament God commands that His people take periodic times off, gather everyone around, and feast for days? One of the stipulations made frequently is that this be done "in My Presence."

Why? *Because God enjoys watching us enjoy what He has blessed us with.* God often uses the metaphor "Father" to describe His relationship with us. He is the

model of the perfect parent. Since He enjoys His children, you can be sure we were meant to enjoy ours.

It is important to take your eyes off what everyone else
has and refocus them on God. That frees you up so you
can enjoy what God has given you. Use those things He
has given you. Use them up. Share them with others. Involve as many as you can in appreciating God's blessings.

4. *God*

God wants to have a vital, meaningful, fulfilling relationship with you. Christ died so people could have such
a relationship with God. Our guilt has been taken away,
and as we come to God through faith, the relationship
we have with God is based on grace, not guilt. This relationship should be one you enjoy, not one you endure.
Set aside everything else and open your arms to receive
that relationship. As you do, you will demonstrate to
your kids what it means to be a real man—or woman.

Live for a Greater Purpose

The Lord wants us to get our eyes off the unimpor-
tant things of life and see the bigger picture, the purposes He has for our lives. But too often we get caught up in
what the world thinks is important and miss the mark
God has for our lives. He has good works He has foreor-
dained for us to walk in. Seek Him for this, and ask Him
to show You things from His perspective. When you do
this, things that once seemed so important will almost
become laughable, like the struggle of keeping up with
the Joneses. As we shall see in a moment, we are to seek
His kingdom first, and He will add anything we need
that the Joneses now have.

JESUS' BLUEPRINT
FOR CONTENTMENT

Matthew 6:31–33 says:

"So do not worry, saying, 'What shall we eat?' or 'What shall we drink?' or 'What shall we wear?' For the pagans run after all these things, and your heavenly Father knows that you need them. But seek first his kingdom and his righteousness, and all these things will be given to you as well."

We weren't created to get satisfaction out of things. Deep in the heart of every person is an awareness that we are on this planet for a purpose greater than

- having a career,
- paying our bills,
- loving our families, or
- fulfilling our roles as upstanding citizens.

When the motive is not right, even going to church and attempting to worship God can leave us feeling something's missing.

Jesus gives us the way to reach a higher purpose than the mundane, discontented way of life so many are trapped in. *But seek first his kingdom.* The word *kingdom* was a popular phrase in Jesus' day. It means "the realm over which God's kingship is tangibly demonstrated."

Asked differently: "What would it look like if God were in charge of Los Angeles (or your city)?" In part it would look like heaven on earth. He would rule with absolute fairness and justice, yet with mercy and compassion.

Take a minute now and work through the same thought process on the three following areas. Why would they be different? What could you do right now to make some of that difference true in your life and relationships? In Jesus' kingdom?

- Imagine how relationships would be.
- Imagine how people would respond toward others in need.
- Imagine how business transactions would be.

Next, Jesus says to *seek*. Nancy and I have the goal of seeking to demonstrate this kind of life in our world. We want to make our home one in which God is in charge and in which His order is seen. In the areas of our friendships, business, and community involvement, we seek to show forth Jesus and to be a light to those in darkness. As part of that, we want to spread His influence to those around us so that His kingdom will be evident in the lives of all with whom we come in contact.

When Jesus said *first,* He was indicating that we are to make the seeking of His kingdom the absolute priority of our lives. That's a tall order when you consider how many things demand our time. But the Lord says that when we put Him first, then all the things that might have been put ahead of Him will turn out right: *"All these things will be given to you as well."*

So, what are you living for? God has a mission He wants to involve each of us in. As you look at the next few years, be certain you are in the center of God's mission for your life. As a part of that, in whatever you are doing, you will want to seek first God's kingdom by expressing His love, truth, and grace.

As you obey, you will start seeing some of the greater

purposes God has for your life, purposes that go far beyond what you would have thought of by yourself. His purposes always have eternal value. Ours too often do not.

As you do this, you will discover that nothing strikes at the core of the grass-is-greener syndrome better than obeying God. What a joy it is to give yourself up to Him and His purpose for your life. This is the way to live in contentment and let the tent of discontentment remain in your past.

Notes

1. Glen Martin, *Beyond the Rat Race* (Nashville: Broadman & Holman, 1995), 32.
2. Ibid., 32.
3. Ibid., 31.
4. Max Anders, *The Good Life* (Dallas: Word, 1993), 11.

chapter twelve

The Benefits of God's Top Ten List

Fear the Lord your God, serve him only.

—Deuteronomy 6:13

Two views of the commandments are all too common today. People either add to them, implying that God was the author of all of the "Thou shalts" and "Thou shalt nots" of human invention, or they discount the applicability of His Top Ten by saying they were for another era, not today. John Leo writes,

> These are dark days for the Ten Commandments. It's not just that people go around breaking them all the time (nothing new there), but that so few of us seem able to remember what these oft-broken rules actually say. In 1994, a survey of 1,200 people, ages fifteen to thirty-five, found that most of those polled could name no more than two commandments, and as the essayist Cullen Murphy writes, "They weren't too happy about some of the others when they were told about them."[1]

Today people do not want to be told what to do. Not that they really ever did, but since the rebellious years of the sixties, laws have been something most want to break or avoid at all costs. Doing it "my way" is the way of choice for most people.

One study I came across revealed not only how little we know about God's Top Ten List, but also how few follow them. A large proportion of the respondents (64–95 percent, depending on the commandment) said that they personally followed the Ten Commandments. They didn't curse or use profanity, they respected their parents; they didn't commit murder or adultery, or steal, or lie about other persons, or envy what they had. But when it came to what the respondents thought their neighbors did, it was a different matter. Only 15 percent thought the majority of Americans cursed and used profanity; only 22 percent thought the majority attended a house of worship regularly and refrained from envying the things someone else had. Only 49 percent of the respondents thought Americans in general worshiped the true God. The percentages were better for the rest of the list, but they still weren't high.[2]

WHY WE STILL NEED GOD'S TOP TEN LIST

Many today are a little perplexed about a return to the basics. You may be one. God never intended for His commandments to make our lives miserable. He gave them because they reflected His character and because they were essential. Following them would allow us to experience the freedom of the life He intended. So let's look at three benefits of the Ten Commandments for your life as we approach the next millennium.

They Hold Up a Mirror of the Real You

God's Top Ten List represents a measuring stick for life. It is a picture of the very character of God. So, as

God reveals His holiness and expectation for perfection, we discover just how far we fall short and in turn are driven into the loving arms of the Lord Jesus Christ. As we see our shortfalls, this encourages us to allow the Holy Spirit to change us. After all, the Scripture says that we are being changed into the image of Jesus. This is a process only God can carry out successfully as we allow His Spirit to make us more like Jesus. This means sanding off the rough edges of our nature. As we feel God's heavenly sandpaper in the form of problems or correction, we should not complain or resist, but instead should rejoice. For this shows that God loves us so much that He is willing to discipline us. We don't really want to hold on to ungodly actions anyway, if we desire to live a pleasing, holy life.

This is why He encourages us in Hebrews 12:5–7, "'My son, do not make light of the Lord's discipline, and do not lose heart when he rebukes you, because the Lord disciplines those he loves, and he punishes everyone he accepts as a son. Endure hardship as discipline. God is treating you as sons. For what son is not disciplined by his father?" Discipline is not fun at the time, but it brings the best fruit in the long run. God's discipline really is like spiritual pruning. It produces better fruit afterward.

They Are a Deterrent to Evil

Because we live with such an uncertainty of ethics and morals, Leith Anderson wisely asks, "Could it be that the divisiveness among Christians comes from failure to define what are truly Christian values?"[3] James William McClendon writes, "The Ten Commandments seem not to have fared well in recent Christianity. Though the giving of the law at Sinai remains as a colorful part of the story Christians tell, there seems to be a sense that the Ten Words belong to the past."[4] Obviously, as long as evil is alive and well and we live outside any moral framework, we will continue to slide down the slippery slope of morality. Our entire judicial system, with its millions of laws, was all originally designed to enforce God's Top Ten List. But even as I write this, one judge in Alabama is fighting a court decision against his right to have the Ten Commandments on the wall of his courtroom.

They Give a Framework for Life

Although the law does not give the power to obey it (only God through the Holy Spirit can do that), it helps us by revealing when we fall short of God's standards. It motivates us to want to live more successfully for God, with a game plan that really works. That's because God knows our nature and what we need to live successfully. He's on our side when He gives these commands, rather than being the cosmic killjoy so many today mistakenly think Him to be. Those who have the Ten Commandments as their standard for life are never disappointed.

God is gracious in supplying the believer with power to live within those guidelines, as Paul reminds us in Philippians 4:13, "I can do everything through him who gives me strength."

LET'S GET PRACTICAL

Too often we see the Ten Commandments as a set of Hebrew words, inscribed on stone tablets, ancient and unusable. Let's get very practical and penetrate our present-day lives. What should you take with you from this book? Head knowledge is abundant in an informational age. It's time for this information to travel the eighteen to twenty inches to our hearts. What does God's Top Ten List mean to me *this week?*

Commandment #1: Accept No Substitute

You've already learned how to give God first place in your life. Don't let anything steal your devotion. Paul wrote to the church in Corinth, "But I am afraid that just as Eve was deceived by the serpent's cunning, your minds may somehow be led astray from your sincere and pure devotion to Christ" (2 Corinthians 11:3). Never allow anything to substitute for God's central place in your life.

Commandment #2: Refuse to Reduce God

It is so easy to reduce God to mental or physical images that "limit" His limitless existence, power, and glory. Ezekiel 14:7 says, "When any Israelite or any alien living in Israel separates himself from me and sets up idols in his heart and puts a wicked stumbling block before his face and then goes to a prophet to inquire of me, I the Lord will answer him myself.'" The indication from this verse is that idolatry begins in the heart. Guard your heart. Refuse to reduce God.

Commandment #3: Take God Seriously

God's name is important. His name represents His character and His reputation. The ungodly use His name in vain (Psalm 74:10). But if we respect our Lord, we will be very careful with how we use His name. The godly person will follow David's example in Psalm 86:11–12, where he states, "Teach me your way, O Lord, and I will walk in your truth; give me an undivided heart, that I may fear your name. I will praise you, O Lord my God, with all my heart; I will glorify your name forever."

Commandment #4: Honor God's Day of Rest

God rested after He completed the Creation. "God blessed the seventh day and made it holy, because on it he rested from all the work of creating that he had done" (Genesis 2:3). This day of rest is a time when we can remember God's goodness to us and His complete provision for our needs. It is a day when we especially put Him first. It is also a time for rest and recuperation after the toil of the week. Jesus' words in Mark 6:31 to His disciples are also a loving invitation to us: "Come with me by yourselves to a quiet place and get some rest."

God considered this day of rest so important, that He told the people of Israel that delighting in this holy day was linked to their prosperity as a nation.

"If you keep your feet from breaking the Sabbath and from doing as you please on my holy day, if you call the Sabbath a delight and the Lord's holy day honorable, and if you honor it by not going your own way and not doing as you please or speaking idle words, then you will find your joy in the Lord, and I will cause you to ride on the heights of the land." (Isaiah 58:13–14)

Commandment #5: Honor Your Parents

You don't need to honor all their practices, but you must honor their position. Learn to appreciate those who represent the most influential relationship in your life. When you do, you can expect the promise of Ephesians 6:3 to be yours: "that it may go well with you and that you may enjoy long life on the earth." Honoring them brings blessings to you as well.

Commandment #6: Control Your Anger

We are commanded not to murder, and Jesus taught that keeping this commandment included even murderous thoughts about our neighbor or denigration of him. Ephesians 4:26 says, "'In your anger do not sin.' Do not let the sun go down while you are still angry." You will have times of anger in your life. Remember the consequences, and daily ask the Lord to give you His control. Then, when you do get angry, deal with it *immediately,* asking the Lord for help so that your feelings of anger do not spill over into sin. If they do, confess the sin right away and let the Holy Spirit give you His control once more.

Commandment #7: Affair-Proof Your Marriage

God's standard is clear. One mate—one lifetime. Commit to God's ideal of sexual purity. The rewards are worth it. The rewards include a clean conscience, no fear of getting a sexually transmitted disease, and many others. But realize that you will be working on this one all your life—working to strengthen your relationship with your mate and consciously avoiding anything that might lead you into temptation.

Commandment #8: Manage Your Money Wisely

We are commanded not to steal, and that includes using our money ethically and not letting worry over finances cause us to grasp after gain. How you handle your money will greatly influence the climate of your whole life. When you spend every penny you have and more, you create stress and are never satisfied. You are probably always uptight that a medical condition might arise, or that there will be a breakdown in your car or appliances, or that you will have unexpected home repairs or an accident or some other emergency that you will not be able financially to meet. Even the need periodically to replace your vehicle can produce tension. When such stress is present there also is a wall built up between you and God, since you are not living according to His leading. Learning to live in contentment with what you have will go a long, long way toward reducing the setbacks and any barriers finances have caused to be erected between you and the Lord.

If you don't manage your money wisely, you will be enslaved to debt. God calls us to freedom and shows us the way to manage our money wisely. Bring Him into developing a workable budget and then allow Him to help you stay on it. Involving Him also in the decision for nonessential purchases is a good practice to avoid unnecessary buying.

Commandment #9: Tell the Truth

We are commanded not to give false testimony about our neighbor, and that includes being a person of absolute integrity in every area—legal, business, and personal. Truth is the solid foundation of any relationship. Jesus is Truth. So when we have Him in our lives, it is easier to be truthful than when we do not. He is the key to living the Christian life successfully. Truth can be a way of life for us when we ask Him daily to help us be honest and truthful in every area of life we will encounter in the coming day.

Commandment #10: Learn to Be Content

Satan coveted God's glory and fell from heaven. Cain coveted God's approval, and killed his brother. David coveted Uriah's wife, and committed murder and adultery. *We* covet our neighbor's home, spouse, belongings, servants—all that the Lord has blessed him with—and sometimes we end up murdering our neighbor or sleeping with his spouse. The apostle Paul said that even if we manage to obey all the other commandments, we will surely fall in this one, for it is so natural for us to envy someone else's blessing.

Enjoy and appreciate the incredible provisions God has for you. To live in discontentment is to question God's goodness and to set yourself up for missing so much that God has for you. Jesus said, "I am come that they might have life, and that they might have it more abundantly" (John 10:10 KJV). Draw on the peace of Jesus and be as Paul, who learned to be content in whatever situation he found himself because he knew his God and had learned to trust Him 100 percent. When we trust someone that completely, knowing He is in control, we are able to relax and find contentment no matter what is going on around us.

OUR RESPONSE

I have officiated at well over one hundred weddings. Despite subtle changes in vows and musical arrangements, all of the weddings I have performed see a bride and a groom pledging to remain faithful to each other "until death do us part." Yet the fire sometimes dwindles over the years, and many of these couples end up in a pastor's or counselor's office struggling to remain faithful. The change was never a sudden thing. Typically, it begins gradually—perhaps when one partner fails to put the laundry in the hamper, or when one person squeezes the toothpaste from the middle, or even when one partner is unwilling to share the remote control—and then love becomes a distant remembrance of a better time.

What the partners once did to win the love of their mates, they no longer do to keep their love.

Any couple that has been married for a long time will tell you life isn't always a fairy tale. There are tremendous highs and depressing lows—all a part of two people "cleaving" together. Hardships are overcome, pain is shared, and hurts are experienced together. But veteran couples say the same thing: "It has been worth it!" All they mean by those five words is this: The long-term benefits of faithfulness always outweigh the short-sighted gains found in ditching the love of their life. Perseverance is worth it! Endurance is worth it!

Those two words, *perseverance* and *endurance,* are found throughout the Bible where faithfulness is mentioned. Like any marriage, your relationship with God will be marked sometimes by hardships and headaches. There will be low times when you wake up and don't feel like being a Christian, times when you will be tempted to give up on God's Top Ten List for some shortsighted gain or experience. If your love for God is solely based on warm feelings, then any change in mood or circumstances can destroy your passion for your Savior. Yet, where faithfulness is maintained, where you set your eyes upon the long run, not the short sprint, the Christian life becomes a joyous pilgrimage. The book of Hebrews says, "Therefore, since we are surrounded by such a great cloud of witnesses, let us throw off everything that hinders and the sin that so easily entangles, and let us run with perseverance the race marked out for us" (Hebrews 12:1). One of the fruits of our faithfulness to God is the ability to complete this most difficult race and capture the extravagant rewards that God has promised. The Spirit of God longs for us to be Christlike, and so be fulfilled. He wants the character of God to be evident in our lives. He wants for Christ to live in us and guide our days.

> Trust in the Lord and do good;
>> dwell in the land and enjoy safe pasture.
> Delight yourself in the Lord
>> and he will give you the desires of your heart.
>> (Psalm 37:3–4)

Notes

1. John Leo, "Thou Shalt Not Command," *U.S. News & World Report,* 18 November 1996, 16.
2. Roger Rosenblatt, "The 11th Commandment: Whatever Happened to 'Love thy neighbor'?" *Family Circle,* 21 December 1993, 30.
3. Leith Anderson, *Winning the Values War in a Changing Culture* (Minneapolis: Bethany, 1994), 32.
4. James McClendon, *Ethics* (Nashville: Abingdon, 1986), 177.

REVIEW AND STUDY GUIDE

James S. Bell Jr.

Chapter One

1. Our culture does not want moral absolutes, and that is why we are in a moral crisis.

2. Secularism, pluralism, and privatization all espouse the idea that there are many truths and that your own beliefs are as valid as anyone else's.

3. God wanted a deeper relationship with His people Israel so He gave them ten foundational principles to obey that reflect His character.

4. When we see God's words and actions as loving and trustworthy we realize His commandments will lead us in the right direction.

5. The commandments make crystal clear what sin is universally, and all of us, believers or not, recognize their truth.

6. Only through Jesus Christ can we understand the full meaning of the commandments and have the power to keep them.

Questions and Response

1. Make up your own top ten list about why it is difficult to keep various commandments.

2. What do you think is the greatest thing the Law can accomplish? What is the most important thing it fails to do?

Chapter Two

1. We often explain away consequences in our life by changing our terminology to soft-pedal our failures.

2. God alone sets the standards for greatness, so our commitments should reflect His priorities.

3. There is greater gain in learning from the mistakes of others rather than suffering due to our own ignorance.

4. Our priorities demonstrate what is closest to our hearts, and if God is first in our lives, He will supply all our other needs.

5. Our abilities can be greatly used by God, but the more we have, the greater is the temptation to think of ourselves as independent of Him.

6. God is completely trustworthy and faithful, but we often fail to risk much in living according to His high standards.

QUESTIONS AND RESPONSE

1. Review all the major roles, responsibilities, and resources in your life. Where do you succeed in putting God first? Where do you fail?

2. In what areas of your life do you see yourself acting as a manager of God's resources? In what areas do you see yourself as the owner?

Chapter Three

1. Our culture is largely ignorant of the true God, and He is often reduced to a form and stature that makes us comfortable and less accountable.

2. Worshiping a golden calf in the shadow of Mount Sinai demonstrated how far removed the gods of our making are from the true God.

3. God-substitutes fall into four general categories: possessions, reputation, others, and self. Though we try to use them, we actually worship and serve them.

4. Images of God always fail because they are deficient in showing His glory and fully expressing His nature. God is not localized or able to be controlled.

5. We cannot understand God unless we obey His commands, which is synonymous with loving Him.

6. There is fulfillment, freedom, and hope for the future if we worship God in the way He has provided, but this requires surrender and devotion.

QUESTIONS AND RESPONSE

1. Take five of God's attributes listed in the chapter and look up the Scripture verses given with those attributes. Describe how each verse typifies that characteristic of God.

2. To what things or people do you ascribe some of the above characteristics that are really God's alone? Make a plan to resist this tendency.

Chapter Four

POINTS TO CONSIDER

1. God has a seemingly endless list of names that reveal His many characteristics, attributes, and qualities to His people through Scripture.

2. Biblical characters' names reflected their behavior, personality, or actions, rather than merely being an arbitrary label.

3. We not only see God's nature in His names, but His close presence, His accomplishments, and how He relates to us.

4. God's name can be used to illegitimately justify our own wrong behavior or as a weapon to use against others.

5. Our lives are crowded with the presence of God—at work in all of our trials and our joys.

QUESTIONS AND RESPONSE

1. In what ways have you misused God's name, even if it is not as serious as profanity? How might you better respect His name by your words and deeds?

2. Where do you most lack a sense of God's presence, especially when you are alone or are in the midst of various trials? Confess His presence and power in these areas of your life.

Chapter Five

Points to Consider

1. Burnout is not restricted to old age, but reflects the stressful lifestyles many of us lead.

2. A moderate level of stress may be beneficial, but too much takes a terrible toll on our health, job, and family.

3. To remember the Sabbath means not only to go to church but to take life easier, to relax, and to recreate.

4. We sometimes run away from the Sabbath because it does not satisfy flawed personal needs or desires; for example, the desire for too much or the perception of not enough, especially in the material realm.

5. The lack of commitment to the Lord's Day has adverse consequences in the whole person—physical, mental, and spiritual.

6. A time of rest allows us to refocus our purpose, to analyze our performance, and to adjust our goals. The Sabbath allows for this.

Questions and Response

1. Would you say you have the rest that Jesus promises? Where in the Scripture do you see warnings against overwork?

2. Analyze the way you have spent Sundays in the last few months. How would you rate yourself in terms of the quality of your worship and the quality of your rest?

Chapter Six

POINTS TO CONSIDER

1. Honoring our parents as children means that we obey and respect them, whereas when we are adults it means that we value and care for them.

2. Becoming independent of our parents does not mean we should cast them away, but that we should seek interdependence and receive their input.

3. Parenting itself is an honorable calling—much more so than our careers or other skills—yet society has devalued it.

4. We should not only honor our parents but become honorable parents ourselves, by living morally and spiritually according to God's standards.

5. We may appreciate our parents but unless we express it in tangible ways they may rarely experience it.

6. Most of us have at least some unresolved conflict with our parents that needs to be reconciled, and we should make every effort to achieve it.

QUESTIONS AND RESPONSE

1. Make up your own top ten list of ways to honor your parents and choose at least two you can perform in the next week.

2. List both the weaknesses and strengths inherited from your parents. Forgive them for the weaknesses and praise them for the strengths.

Chapter Seven

1. The command not to murder not only includes refraining from killing the body but also refraining from doing anything that harms the soul or spirit of a person.

2. When we degrade or devalue someone, we are in effect denegrating God because we reject His image in that person.

3. Anger improperly expressed cannot be excused and has many damaging effects to both self and others.

4. Rage, repression, resentment, and revenge are typical ways we express anger, but repentance and restoration are essential for change in this area.

5. We are capable of touching others deep within their soul to bring encouragement and healing amidst pain and brokenness.

6. The minor issues and annoyances of life should not be part of the legacy by which we are remembered.

QUESTIONS AND RESPONSE

1. Think back to your last outburst of destructive anger. What wrong approaches triggered it, and what were the negative results? How can you change this in the future?

2. Follow the author's practical suggestions and make amends with those you've hurt by seeking their forgiveness and affirming them in creative ways.

Chapter Eight

1. We may not realize our differences as men and women, but we do have different needs that must be met to achieve a close relationship.

2. If these different needs aren't met by our spouse, physical intimacy may fail, and the chances for an affair increase.

3. Adultery begins in the heart, not in the act, and impure thoughts alone have their own negative consequences.

4. Taking responsibility in marriage means complete fidelity to your mate. If you fail, you need to move immediately toward confession and restoration.

5. We need to keep appropriate boundaries—physical, emotional, circumstantial—with members of the opposite sex who are not our spouse.

6. Maximizing your marriage means being committed to all of your spouse's needs and working through the difficult issues.

QUESTIONS AND RESPONSE

1. Discuss with your spouse the list of particular needs you each have. How can you mutually meet each other's needs more effectively?

2. Reread the top ten reasons for avoiding an affair. Which ones have you never thought of that might help you in times of temptation?

Chapter Nine

1. Stealing goes beyond directly taking what does not belong to you and includes many forms of evading or withholding.

2. Complete honesty always pays off in terms of a clear conscience, how God views us, and the rewards that follow.

3. Greed, laziness, and pride cause us to short-circuit the difficult process of honesty because we try to get what we want faster with less integrity.

4. We presume a lot when it comes to finances—we don't often know where our money goes or if we can pay our debts in the future.

5. Our checkbook stubs are a good indication of the priorities in our lives and what is closest to our hearts.

QUESTIONS AND RESPONSE

1. This chapter lists four ways of being dishonest besides outright stealing. How would you rate yourself in these and similar actions?

2. What is your response to tithing based on the author's arguments? Pray about how to increase your giving toward or beyond the tithe.

Chapter Ten

1. Lying has two major negative consequences. It does harm to those with whom we are in relationship and it damages our integrity.

2. Our conscience is not a defect keeping us from experiencing our full potential but an indicator of guilt based on our misdeeds.

3. We lie for many different reasons, but the motivation is always to gain an unfair advantage.

4. In order to bridge the gap between greater knowledge of truth and the way we live our lives, we need a commitment to ruthless honesty.

5. As you spend more time in God's Word, which is truth itself, it will be more difficult to be dishonest.

6. It is difficult to be totally honest because we feel God won't support us if we take a radical stand for truth in everything.

Questions and Response

1. When it comes to the five categories of lying found in the chapter, which one most fits your motivation? Get to the root cause of these tactics and give it to the Lord.

2. Find three places in Scripture where lying occurs. What was God's response and what does that say about the importance of honesty?

Chapter Eleven

POINTS TO CONSIDER

1. We often judge happiness based on what others have, and the stress of competition causes us to covet.

2. Always wanting more is symptomatic of our decade, because we are programmed to be discontent with what we have.

3. Besides discontent, in our never-ceasing quest for more we exhaust ourselves, pile up debt, clash with others, and worry about the surplus.

4. Rather than focusing on the next acquisition, we need to consciously thank God for what we have and use— and enjoy it.

5. When we compare ourselves with others, even if we like them, we distance ourselves out of jealousy, inadequacy, or frustration.

QUESTIONS AND RESPONSE

1. Come up with a plan to do one thing to better enjoy what God has given you in the following categories: your spouse, your children, your possessions, your God.

2. How can seeking the rule of God in our homes help to set us free from coveting? Consecrate everything you have for His use.

Chapter Twelve

1. Not keeping or even being *aware* of the commandments is a form of rebellion, which never leads to peace or happiness.

2. If we want a valid measurement of our spiritual condition we should view our lives in light of God's Top Ten List—the Ten Commandments.

3. The commandments call us to place God in first place and to deal with others in a manner consistent with His character.

4. As statistics show, we feel we are more righteous in our living than the majority of Americans, but this is rarely the case.

5. The measure of our relationship to God is not based on high or low feelings but rather on obedience to His commands enabled by His grace.

6. There are great rewards for those who run the race and remain faithful to God's laws. Persevere always, and with God's help you'll see success.

QUESTIONS AND RESPONSE

1. We invent many religious rules when God gave only ten. Name some of these human regulations that God Himself may not require.

2. If the Ten Commandments represent a framework for successful living, which ones especially do you need to work on to please God and live a more fruitful life?

3. Name one or more new insights this book has given you into the meaning and implication of the various commandments.

Moody Press, a ministry of Moody Bible Institute, is designed for education, evangelization, and edification. If we may assist you in knowing more about Christ and the Christian life, please write us without obligation: Moody Press, c/o MLM, Chicago, Illinois 60610.